Beginning PHP

Master the latest features of PHP 7 and fully embrace
modern PHP development

David Carr

Markus Gray

BIRMINGHAM - MUMBAI

Beginning PHP

Acquisitions Editor: Koushik Sen
Content Development Editor: Murtaza Haamid
Production Coordinator: Samita Warang

First published: July 2018

Production reference: 1300718

Published by Packt Publishing Ltd.
Livery Place
35 Livery Street
Birmingham B3 2PB, UK.

ISBN 978-1-78953-590-7

www.packtpub.com

https://mapt.packtpub.com/

Mapt is an online digital library that gives you full access to over 5,000 books and videos, as well as industry leading tools to help you plan your personal development and advance your career. For more information, please visit https://mapt.packtpub.com/ website.

Why Subscribe?

- Spend less time reading and more time coding with practical eBooks and Videos from over 4,000 industry professionals
- Improve your learning with Skill Plans built especially for you
- Get a free eBook or video every month
- Mapt is fully searchable
- Copy and paste, print, and bookmark content

PacktPub.com

Did you know that Packt offers eBook versions of every book published, with PDF and ePub files available? You can upgrade to the eBook version at www.PacktPub.com and as a print book customer, you are entitled to a discount on the eBook copy. Get in touch with us at service@packtpub.com for more details.

At www.PacktPub.com, you can also read a collection of free technical articles, sign up for a range of free newsletters, and receive exclusive discounts and offers on Packt books and eBooks.

Contributors

About the Authors

David Carr, for the past 12 years, has been developing applications for the web, using mostly PHP. He does this for a living and loves what he does as every day there is something new and exciting to learn.

David often attends PHP conferences and attends local meetups to learn and teach others.

He spends a lot of time learning new techniques and actively helping other people learn web development through a variety of help groups. He also writes web development tutorials for his website and blog about advancements in web design and development. You can read more about him here: https://daveismyname.blog/.

Markus Gray is a full-stack web developer/designer with 11 years' experience, based in Philadelphia.

He has diverse and deep interests in most trending technologies. He spends most of his time helping public and private companies, and has also worked with the federal government in the department of education. Currently, he is the CEO of Syncware Technologies, Inc. He is extremely passionate about teaching, and hopes to spend more and more time helping young developers in the community become proficient at software development.

Packt Is Searching for Authors like You

If you're interested in becoming an author for Packt, please visit authors.packtpub.com and apply today. We have worked with thousands of developers and tech professionals, just like you, to help them share their insight with the global tech community. You can make a general application, apply for a specific hot topic that we are recruiting an author for, or submit your own idea.

Table of Contents

Preface

Developing a website is a priority these days in order for your business to have a presence on the internet. Design and development are foundational steps for any website. PHP is commonly used for website and web application development. PHP is a general purpose, server-side scripting language that's designed to make dynamic pages and applications. PHP as a web development option is secure, fast, and reliable, and also offers lots more advantages that make it accessible to a lot of people. We should consider what has made PHP one of the most widely used programming languages in the web industry.

This book gets you up to speed by starting with basic concepts, such as variables, data types, arrays, and loops. It then progresses to more advanced concepts, such as building your own frameworks and creating your app.

The book has been designed for the purpose of reducing the gap between learning and implementation. It provides a lot of real business case scenarios, which will help you to understand the concepts and get started with writing PHP programs as soon as they complete the book.

What This Book Covers

Chapter 1, Getting Started with PHP, covers the fundamentals of using the PHP programming language. In this chapter, you'll learn basic PHP syntax and program structure. You'll also learn how to use variables, data types, operators, and conditionals.

Chapter 2, Arrays and Loops, shows you how to use the flow control structures. We will specifically cover loops and arrays in this chapter.

Chapter 3, *Functions and Classes*, teaches you to identify how to define and call functions. We will also cover how to create classes, and how to use the classes and functions together.

Chapter 4, *Data Operations*, teaches you how to handle input from users and printing outcomes back to them, handling errors gracefully, and learning the basics of using the MySQL database.

Chapter 5, *Building a PHP Web Application*, teaches you to apply OOP concepts in a framework. We will cover error reporting using the Whoops library and will learn how to handle those errors. We will also cover how to manage and structure our application in a framework.

Chapter 6, *Building a PHP Framework*, teaches you to build an MVC framework from scratch. Starting from an empty directory, we will build an entire working framework as a starting point for more complex applications.

Chapter 7, *Authentication and User Management*, teaches you the security aspect of the project, that is, authentication. We will be building login forms which interact with the database to verify the identity of the users. We will also cover how to set up a password recovery mechanism in our application.

Chapter 8, *Building a Contacts Management System*, teaches you to build a contacts CRUD (Create, Read, Update, and Delete) section, which will have a view page to view an individual contact. We will also be building the comments system for our contact application.

What You Need for This Book

Hardware

The minimum hardware requirements are as follows:

- Windows 7 64-bit
- Processor: Intel Core processor
- Memory: 1 GB RAM
- An internet connection

Software

- WAMP server for Windows

- LAMP server for Linux

- MAMP server for Mac

- Browser: the latest version of one or more browsers (Internet Explorer 11, or Chrome 54.0.2840 or newer is recommended)

- A text editor such as Notepad or Notepad++

Who This Book Is For

This book is for anyone interested in learning the fundamentals of PHP programming. For the best experience, you should have basic knowledge of HTML, CSS, JavaScript, and MySQL.

Conventions

In this book, you will find a number of text styles that distinguish between different kinds of information. Here are some examples of these styles and an explanation of their meaning.

Code words in text, database table names, folder names, filenames, file extensions, pathnames, dummy URLs, user input, and Twitter handles are shown as follows: "Create a new file and name it `syntax.php`."

Folder names, filenames, file extensions, pathnames, include file names in text are shown as follows: "To remove an element from an array, use the `unset` function.

A block of code is set as follows:

```php
<?php
  echo "Hello World";
?>
```

Any command-line input or output is written as follows:

```
php syntax.php
```

New terms and important words are shown in bold. Words that you see on the screen, for example, in menus or dialog boxes, appear in the text like this: "So, when we click on the **Submit** button, the data will be submitted."

Important new **programming terms** are shown in bold. *Conceptual terms* are shown in italics.

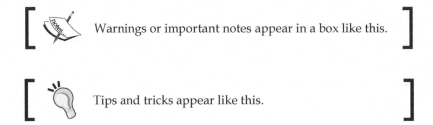

Warnings or important notes appear in a box like this.

Tips and tricks appear like this.

Installation and Setup

Before you start this book, we'll install a PHP server, such as WAMP, and a text editor, such as Atom.

Installing WAMP on Windows

1. Visit http://www.wampserver.com/en/ in your browser.
2. Click on **WAMP SERVER 64 bits** or **WAMP SERVER 32 bits**, depending on your system.
3. Next, there will be a popup, which will give you a couple of warnings. Click on **download directly**.
4. Open the installer after download.
5. Follow the steps in the installer and that's it! Your WAMP server is ready.

Installing LAMP in Linux

1. Visit https://bitnami.com/stack/lamp/installer in your browser.
2. Under **Linux**, click on the **Download** button.
3. Next, there will be a popup, which will give you options for logging in. Just click on **No thanks, just take me to the download** option.
4. Open the installer after download.
5. Follow the steps in the installer and that's it! Your LAMP server is ready.

Installing MAMP for MAC OS

1. Visit https://www.mamp.info/en/ in your browser.
2. Under MAMP, click on **DOWNLOAD** button.
3. In the next page, click on **macOS** click on **Download** button.
4. Open the installer after download.
5. Follow the steps in the installer and that's it! Your MAMP server is ready.

Downloading the Example Code

You can download the example code files from your account at http://www.packtpub.com for all the Packt Publishing books you have purchased. If you purchased this book elsewhere, you can visit http://www.packtpub.com/support and register to have the files e-mailed directly to you.

The code bundle for the book is also hosted on GitHub at https://github.com/TrainingByPackt/Beginning-PHP/. In case there's an update to the code, it will be updated on the existing GitHub repository.

1
Getting Started with PHP

PHP, or Pre-Processor Hypertext, is a programming language that is used to design web applications and to make a website look more intuitive and interesting. PHP has also gained a lot of popularity over the years as a server-side scripting language. PHP is an easy to use, but powerful, language. PHP works on multiple operating systems and can support multiple servers. All of these features of PHP make it an ideal candidate for a web designing language.

This book will take you through the basics of PHP, including declaring the syntax, declaring and using the variables and data types, operators, and conditionals. It will then cover the principles of building a PHP framework along with building your own PHP web application.

In this chapter, you will begin to learn the building blocks of the PHP programming language. We will be covering the syntax and how to declare and use variables in PHP. We will also look at controlling the execution flow using the if statement.

By the end of this chapter, you should be able to write simple programs using these elements.

By the end of this chapter, you will be able to:

- Use the basic syntax of PHP to write simple programs
- Use variables for different data, and manipulate them using different operators
- Use conditionals to control the flow of execution

The Basics

We will start our journey with a look at PHP syntax and executing our first file. Let's begin.

In PHP, syntax is very important; you need proper syntax for your server to know where it should start parsing PHP, and you have to show it via the open and close PHP tags, as shown here:

```
<?php

?>
```

Through using the PHP tags, you can add your code just about anywhere in the document. This means that if you have an HTML website, you can just add the tags, along with some PHP code, and it will process. In addition to using the open and close PHP tags, you must also use the `.php` extension in your file.

Let's get started with a quick example.

Using PHP to Display "Hello World"

In this section, we are going to use what we've learned so far to display a string to the user:

1. Open your code editor.
2. Create a new file and name it `syntax.php`.
3. Enter the following, and save your document:

   ```
   <?php

   ?>
   ```

4. Open your working directory in the **Terminal.**
5. Type the following command:

   ```
   php syntax.php
   ```

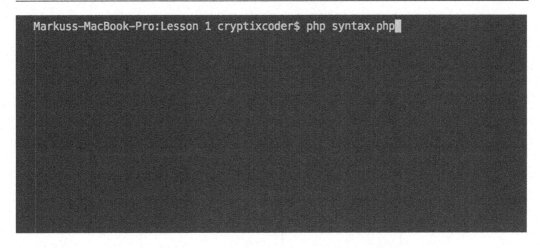

```
Markuss-MacBook-Pro:Lesson 1 cryptixcoder$ php syntax.php
```

6. Switch back to your document and enter the following:

```php
<?php
    echo "Hello World";
?>
```

7. Go back to the Terminal and type the following:

```
php syntax.php
```

You should now see the string, "Hello World" printed on the screen.

Variables and Data Types

To start our learning with PHP, we must first look at the core building blocks that will be used to build every project. In our applications, we will always need a way to store our data temporarily (in our case, we call the storage methods variables).

Variables are defined as follows:

```
$VARIABLENAME = "VALUE";
```

As you can see in the preceding example, variables start off using the $ symbol, followed by the name, and the value is assigned using the assignment operator. Here, we have a variable named VARIABLENAME, with a string value of VALUE.

Variable names cannot start with numbers or special symbols, besides the $ sign, used to define the variable itself.

PHP is one of the few languages that doesn't require you to declare a data type before assigning a value.

Types	Examples
String	"Hello World"
Number	123
Float	1.095
Boolean	TRUE or FALSE

We will now try to implement variables in PHP.

Working with Variables

In this section, we will illustrate a real-world example of using variables in a program. We will start off by creating a variable to store a user's name:

1. Open your code editor.

2. Create a new file and name it `variables.php`.

3. Enter the following, and save your document:

```php
<?php
    $name = "John Doe";
    $age = 25;
    $hourlyRate = 10.50;
    $hours = 40;
    echo $name . " is " . $age . " years old.\n";
    echo $name . " makes $" . $hourlyRate . " an hour. \n";
    echo $name . " worked " . $hours . " this week. \n";
?>
```

4. Open your working directory in the Terminal.

5. Enter the following command, and then press *Enter*:

```
Markuss-MacBook-Pro:Lesson 1 cryptixcoder$ php variables.php
John Doe is 25 years old.
John Doe makes $10.5 an hour.
John Doe worked 40 this week.
Markuss-MacBook-Pro:Lesson 1 cryptixcoder$ █
```

> Another way to insert a variable's value into a string is to use this special syntax:
>
> ```php
> <?php
> echo "My name is ${$name}.";
> ?>
> ```

Operators

We will now have a look at the various operators that are available in PHP.

Comparison Operators

In the section on variables, we saw the = symbol, which, in PHP, is known as an assignment operator. This operator does exactly what the name implies, allowing you to give a variable a value. The first operators are known as comparison operators. Comparison operators allow you to compare two values within a given conditional case.

Inside of the set of comparison operators are the equal, identical, not equal, not identical, less than, and greater than operators.

Usage	Name	Description
$a == $b	Equal	TRUE if $a is equal to $b.
$a === $b	Identical	TRUE if $a is equal to $b, and they are of the same type.
$a != $b	Not Equal	TRUE if $a is not equal to $b.
$a !== $b	Not Identical	TRUE if $a is not equal to $b, or they are not of the same type.
$a < $b	Less Than	TRUE if $a is strictly less than $b.
$a > $b	Greater Than	TRUE if $a is strictly greater than $b.
$a <= $b	Less Than or Equal To	TRUE if $a is less than or equal to $b.
$a >= $b	Greater Than or Equal To	TRUE if $a is greater than or equal to $b.

Logical Operators

Up next are logical operators. Logical operators are used to check for multiple cases at one time. The set of logical operators gives you the NOT, AND, and OR operators.

Usage	Name	Description
! $a	NOT	TRUE if $a is not TRUE.
$a && $b	AND	TRUE if both $a and $b are TRUE.
$a || $b	OR	TRUE if either $a or $b is TRUE.

Mathematical Operators

In your program, you will sometimes need to do a little math; this is where mathematical operators come in. They give you the ability to add, subtract, multiply, divide, and get the remainder of two divided numbers.

Usage	Name	Description
$a + $b	Addition	Sum of $a and $b
$a - $b	Subtraction	Difference of $a and $b
$a * $b	Multiplication	Product of $a and $b
$a / $b	Division	Quotient of $a and $b
$a % $b	Modulus	Remainder of $a divided by $b

Let's try to use these operators in PHP.

Combining Variables and Operators

In this section, we will be extending our previous example to calculate the annual salary of our user. Here we go with the steps:

1. Open your code editor.

2. Create a new file and name it `operators.php`.

3. To get started, copy the contents from our `variables.php` document.

4. Now, we will add an additional variable to the document, which will hold the number of weeks:

   ```
   $weeks = 52;
   ```

5. Next, we will use the multiplication operator to calculate our weekly pay and assign it to a new variable:

   ```
   $weeklyPay = $hourlyRate * $hours;
   ```

6. Now, with our weekly pay rate, we can calculate our salary:

   ```
   $salary = $weeks * $weeklyPay;
   ```

7. Our last step is to display our final calculations:

```php
echo $name . " will make $" . $salary . " this year.\n";
```

Your final document should look like the following:

```php
<?php
$name = "John Doe";
$age = 25;
$hourlyRate = 10.50;
$hours = 40;
echo $name . " is " . $age . " years 01d.\n";
echo $name . " makes $" . $hourlyRate . " an hour. \n";
echo $name . " worked " . $hours . " this week.\n";
$weeks = 52;
$weeklypay = $hourlyRate * $hours;
$salary = $weeks * $weeklyPay;
echo $name . " will make $" . $salary . "this year";
?>
```

8. Next, we'll open our directory in our `Terminal` and run the following command:

```
php operators.php
```

9. We should now see our data being displayed:

```
Markuss-MacBook-Pro:Lesson 1 cryptixcoder$ php operators.php
John Doe is 25 years old.
John Doe makes $10.5 an hour.
John Doe worked 40 this week.
John Doe will make $21840 this year.
Markuss-MacBook-Pro:Lesson 1 cryptixcoder$
```

Conditionals

Now that we have a foundation for operators, we can start to use them in what are known as conditionals. Conditionals allow you to control the flow of your program, and they come in the form of `if` statements.

A basic `if` statement is represented as follows:

```
if (conditional){

}
```

Inside of the parentheses, you will hold the condition that is required to activate the code within the curly braces.

Additionally, you can add an `else` statement, which will allow you to give alternate code to run if the condition isn't met:

```
if(conditional){

}
else{

}
```

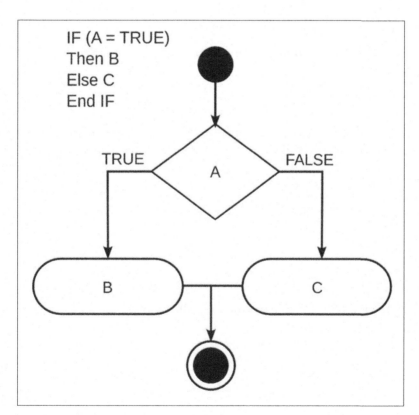

A helpful function to use with conditionals is the `empty` function. The `empty` function is used to check whether a variable is empty

Working with Conditionals

In this section, we will be implementing conditionals where we will check the name of the animal and if it matches, we will be printing the sound of the particular animal.

1. Open your code editor.

2. Create a new file and name it `conditionals.php`.

3. We are going to start by adding our open and close `php` tags:

```php
<?php

?>
```

4. Then, we'll create a new function to hold our animal name:

```php
<?php
    $animal = "cat";
?>
```

5. Now, we can write our first conditional; here, we want to check whether the animal is a cat, and if it is, we will print meow to the user:

```php
<?php
    $animal = "cat";

    if($animal == "cat"){
        echo "meow\n";
    }
?>
```

6. Save the file and open your working directory in the Terminal.

7. Run the following command, and see the results:

```
php conditionals.php
```

```
Markuss-MBP:Lesson 1 cryptixcoder$ php conditionals.php
meow
Markuss-MBP:Lesson 1 cryptixcoder$ █
```

8. Now, we'll expand our conditional a bit further, to add other animal sounds and change our animal to a lion:

```php
$animal = "lion";
if($animal == "cat"){
echo "meow\n";

}
else if ($anima == "dog"){
echo "woof\n";
}

else if($animal == "lion"){
echo "roar\n";

}

else {
echo "What does the fox say?\n";
}

?>
```

9. Now, let's save it again and run the command in the Terminal; you should get the following result:

```
Markuss-MBP:Lesson 1 cryptixcoder$ php conditionals.php
roar
Markuss-MBP:Lesson 1 cryptixcoder$
```

Activity: Building an Employee Salary Calculator

Imagine that you are a PHP developer for a department store chain, and the store is preparing for its upcoming Black Friday sale. Staff who work during the sale hours will be given time and a half, as well as a 10% commission on all sales that they make. Additionally, if they make over $1,000 in gross sales, they will earn a $1,000 bonus. Management wants you to create a calculator that makes it easy for the staff members to calculate how much they earned.

The aim of this activity is to help you understand variables and conditionals.

Follow these steps:

1. Create a new directory and name it `salary_calculator`.
2. Within the new directory, create an `index.php` file.
3. Define the placeholder variables:

```php
<?php

    $hourlyRate = 10.00;
    $hoursWorked = 12;
```

```
$rateMultiplier = 1.5;
$commissionRate = 0.10;
$grossSales = 25.00;
$bonus = 0;
```

4. Our next step will be to define our calculations and assign the outcomes to their respective variables:

```
$holidayRate = $hourlyRate * $rateMultiplier;
    $holidayPay = $holidayRate * $hoursWorked;
    $commission = $commissionRate * $grossSales;
$salary = $holidayPay + $commission;
```

5. Next, we will need to check the gross sales variable to see if the staff member has made over $1,000, to be awarded with a bonus:

```
if($grossSales >= 1000){
        $bonus = 1000;
}
```

6. Now that we have the default rates and the calculators, we can display the results to our user:

```
echo "Salary $" . $salary . "\n";
    echo "Bonus +\$" . $commission . "\n";
    echo "----------------------------\n";
    echo "Total  $" . ($salary + $commission) . "\n";
```

7. All that a staff member would have to do now is change the value of their hourly rate and gross sales and run the program to get their total pay amount.

Summary

We have now reached the end of this chapter. In this chapter, we began with the PHP syntax. We then moved on to variables and the different operators that are used in PHP. Finally, we saw how to implement conditionals and control the execution flow.

You should now have a clear understanding of variables, data types, and conditionals, as well as how they are used together. In the next chapter, you will learn about how arrays and loops are implemented in PHP.

2

Arrays and Loops

In the previous chapter, we covered variables and data types along with the different operators. We also covered how to control the flow of programs using conditionals. In this chapter, we will focus on how to store multiple values using arrays and how to control the flow using loops. The basic idea of an array is that it is a variable type, allowing one to store multiple items within a single `container`.

For example, if you wanted to store the names of all the employees working in a company under the same variable, an array would help you do that. Loops are used when we want to run the same block of code multiple times. This saves a lot of work for the developer by reusing the pre-defined code block. These two concepts are at the core of almost every PHP-based web application and website on the web today.

By the end of this chapter, you will be able to:

- Implement one-dimensional and multidimensional arrays
- Identify the difference between indexed and associative arrays
- Perform different operations on arrays
- Implement various types of loops

Arrays

In this section, we will talk about the various types of arrays and then look at some common operations with them.

Indexed Arrays

Indexed arrays are the most common types of arrays that you will see, and they can be defined as either prepopulated or empty.

An empty array can be defined as follows:

```php
<?php

    $the_array = array();

?>
```

[Note that $the_array is a variable. You can use any other variable that you like.]

Another way to use the shortcut syntax:

```php
<?php
    $the_array = [];
?>
```

If you want to initiate an array with values, you can do so as follows:

```php
<?php

    $students = array("Jill", "Michael", "John", "Sally");

?>
```

When you initialize an array with prepopulated values, each element gets a numeric index, starting at 0. So, in the preceding example, the index for Jill will be 0, the index for Michael will be 1, the index for John will be 2, and the index for Sally will be 3.

In order to print out the first index of the `students` array, you can use the following code:

```php
<?php

    echo $students[0];

?>
```

Usually, when you use an array, you want to add to it throughout the course of your program. This can be done in one of two ways:

The `append` shortcut:

```php
<?php

    $students[] = "Tom";

?>
```

Or the `array_push` function:

```php
<?php

    array_push($students, "Tom", "Joey");

?>
```

Typically, the shortcut method is used by developers; if you want to push multiple records to an array at a time, you can use the `array_push` function.

Sometimes, you'll have an element in an array that needs to be removed. To remove an element from an array, use the `unset` function. In the following example, we remove "Tom" from the array:

```php
<?php

    unset($students[4]);

?>
```

The last section that we will discuss before moving on is updating an element. To do so, do the following:

```php
<?php

    $students[0] = "Jessie";

?>
```

Associative Arrays

Next is associative arrays, better known as key value pairs. With associative arrays, you can use text-based keys to store your values, which can be helpful in specific cases. For example, if we take one of the students from the preceding examples (in this case, Michael), we can store his age, gender, and favorite color, as shown here:

```php
<?php
    $michael = array(
    "age" => 20,
    "gender" => "male",
    "favorite_color" => "blue"
);
?>
```

If you need to access a specific value in the array, you can use the key. For example, if we want to print Michael's age, we can do the following:

```php
<?php

    echo $michael['age'];
?>
```

Adding data to an associative array is just as easy as adding data to an indexed array. You can simply use the key and assign a value. Let's suppose that we want to add an occupation to Michael's array:

```php
<?php
    $michael["occupation"] = "sales associate";
?>
```

To remove an element from an associative array, follow the same steps that we did with the indexed array, but this time, use the key.

Let's remove the occupation that we added in the last step:

```php
<?php
    unset($michael['occupation']);
?>
```

Working with Arrays

In this section, we are going to include name, age, location, and education level. Follow these steps:

1. Open your code editor and create a new file, arrays.php.

2. Within the new file, create your open and close php tags:

    ```php
    <?php

    ?>
    ```

3. Now, we are going to create a new variable, called $myinfo, and initialize it with a new array:

    ```php
    <?php
        $myinfo = array();
    ?>
    ```

4. Then, we are going to populate the new array with our name, age, location, and education level.

5. Next, we'll print our data:

    ```php
    <?php
        $myinfo = array("John", 25, "USA", "College");

        echo "My name is " . $myinfo[0] . "\n";
        echo "I am ". $myinfo[1] . " years old. \n";
        echo "I live in " . $myinfo[2] . "\n";
        echo "My latest education level is " . $myinfo[3];
    ?>
    ```

6. Open your working directory in the Terminal, and type the following command:

    ```
    php arrays.php
    ```

You will get a result as displayed in the following output:

```
My name is John.
I am 25 years old.
I live in USA.
My latest education level is College.
```

Converting a String into an Array

Sometimes, when you're building a PHP-based application, you don't instantiate an array with a predefined set of data - which is the case when building a utility script, for example. Let's suppose that you have a variable with the string version of a filename, and you want to get the name of the file without the extension. This task can be done easily, by using the explode function. The explode function takes two arguments: the delimiter, and the string that you want to convert into an array. Explode function takes two arguments:

```php
<?php
    $filename = "myexamplefile.txt";
    $filename_parts = explode(".", $filename);

    echo "Your filename is " . $filename_parts[0];
?>
```

In the preceding example, we define a filename variable, and then, using the explode function, we break the string into its parts with the period delimiter. The $filename_parts variable contains an array of two elements, the first being the string myexamplefile, and the second containing the string txt.

Knowing this, we can print out the filename by accessing the 0 index of the array of string parts.

Merging an Array into a String

Along with the explode function, PHP also gives us a function that allows us to do the exact opposite: the implode function. When you want to take an existing array and convert it into a string, you can use the implode function to define a delimiter and pass it the array; you'll get a single string as a result.

Let's go back to the `explode` example. Suppose that we have a filename and want to append some other string to the end of it before saving it back to a string:

```php
<?php
    $filename = "myexamplefile.txt";
    $filename_parts = explode(".", $filename);
    $filename_parts[0] .= "_v1";

    $filename = implode(".", $filename_parts);
    echo "Your new filename is " . $filename;

?>
```

In the preceding code example, we start off by using the explode function to break our original filename into its parts. We then access the filename portion and append the string _v1 to the end of it. Using the implode function, we recombine the filename using its parts, and finally, we print it back to the screen for the user to see.

Slicing Arrays

Another `array_slice` function; by default, the function requires only two arguments, but it can take four. The two required arguments are the array itself and the starting point for the new array. The two optional arguments are the length of (or number of elements to include in) the new array and the preserve option. The preserve option allows you to decide whether the current array elements should remain the same, or be reordered after the split. Here's a basic usage example:

```php
<?php
    $fruit = array("apples","grapes", "oranges", "lemons","limes");
    $smallerFruitArray = array_slice($fruit, 2);
?>
```

In the preceding example, when we run the fruit array through `array_slice`, we will get an array containing oranges, lemons, and limes.

Sorting an Array

Sorting is another important tool for building certain types of programs. One of the sorting functions that you'll often see in PHP is the `ksort` function. `ksort` allows you to pass an array in as an argument, and then sort it in ascending order.

An example of how to use it is as follows:

```php
<?php

    $people = array("Jessica" => "35", "April" => "37", "John" =>
"43", "Tom" => 25);
ksort($people);

?>
```

In the preceding example, we have an array of people. Once you put the people array through the `ksort` function, you should see the names in alphabetical order.

Multidimensional Arrays

The next type is the `multidimensional` array. Multidimensional arrays are simply arrays within arrays. In our previous examples of arrays, we stored a student's name. What happens when we want to store multiple details for a specific student? This is where multidimensional arrays come in. Let's look at how we can define a student array that also stores the student's `gender` and `favorite color`:

 For the full code snippet, open the `Lesson 2.php` from the code files.

```php
<?php

    $students = array(
    "Jill" => array(
    "age" => 20,
    "gender" => "female",
....
"Amy" => array(
    "age" => 25,
    "gender" => "female",
    "favorite_color" => "green"
),


);
?>
```

If we want to access a student's information, we can use the following key:

```php
<?php

    echo $students['Jill']['age'];

?>
```

The preceding example will print out Jill's age. With multidimensional arrays, we update element values in pretty much the same way we do when using one-dimensional arrays.

For example, if we want to change Jill's age to 21, we do the following:

```php
<?php

    $students['Jill']['age'] = 21;
?>
```

Including an Array of Hobbies in Our Existing Project

In this section, we are going to expand on the previous example to include an array of hobbies:

1. Open your code editor and create a new file, multidimensional.php.

2. Within the new file, create your open and close php tags.

3. Create a new variable called $user, and initialize it with a new array:

```php
<?php
    ?>
<?php
    $user = array();
?>
```

4. Populate the new array with two main sections: info and hobbies. In the info array, store the name, age, location, and education level, and in the hobbies array, we will store three hobbies.

For the full code snippet, refer to the Lesson 2.php file in the code files folder.

```php
<?php

    $user = array(
      "info" => array(
          "name" => "john",
          "age" => 27,
...

          )
      );

?>
```

5. Next we'll print our data:

For the full code snippet, refer to the Lesson 2.php file in the code files folder.

```php
<?php
    $user = array(
        "info" => array(
            "name" => "john",
            "age" => 27,
            "location" => "USA",
.....
    echo "I live in " . $user["info"]['location'] . ".\n";
    echo "My latest education level is " .
    $user['info']['education_level']. ".\n";

echo "I enjoy " . $user["hobbies"][0] . ", " .
$user["hobbies"]

[1] . ", " . $user["hobbies"][2].".\n";

?>
```

6. Open your working directory in the Terminal and type the following
   command:

```
php multidimensional.php
```

You will get a result based on the input that we provided in the preceding array.

Loops

Loops are powerful tools within any programming language. They allow you
to write code that can be executed a specific number of times, based on a given
condition. In this section, you will learn about the various loops that are available to
you, such as for loops, foreach loops, while loops, and do-while loops.

for Loop

We will start our exploration of loops with the for loop. It is known to be the most
complex loop structure, and it is used when you know how many times you need a
block of code to run. The structure of a for loop is as follows:

```php
<?php

    for(initialized counter; test if true; increment counters){

}

?>
```

The steps to create the for loop are as follows:

1. Initialize the starting count variable - usually, it will start at 0.
2. Provide an evaluation condition that resolves to either true or false. The
   loop will continue if the condition is true, and will exit (or break) when the
   condition is false.
3. Increment the value by a specific number. Typically, it would be incremented
   by 1.

Here's a complete example:

```php
<?php
        for($i = 0; $i < 5; $i++) {
            echo "Current Count: " . $i;
}
?>
```

Combining Loops and Arrays

In this section, we are going to explore how to combine loops and arrays. Here are the steps to do it:

1. Open your code editor and create a new file, `forloop.php`.

2. Within the new file, create your open and close php tags:

    ```
    <?php

    ?>
    ```

3. Now, we create a new variable called `$food`, and initialize it with a new array:

    ```
    <?php

        $food = array();
    ?>
    ```

4. Then, we populate the new array with food names:

    ```
    <?php

        $food = array("turkey", "milk", "apples");
    ?>
    ```

5. Next, we loop through our array and print our data:

    ```
    <?php
        $food = array("turkey", "milk", "apples");

            for($i = 0; $i < count($food); $i++){
        echo $food[$i] . "\n";
    }
    ?>
    ```

 The count function returns the number of elements within an array.

Open your working directory in the Terminal, and type the following command:

```
php forloops.php
```

while Loops

The next loop that we will explore is the while loop. while loops are used when you want to cycle through a block of code until a specific condition is met. while loops are defined as follows:

```php
<?php

    while(condition) {
}

?>
```

while loops are pretty simple, as they only require a condition to run. The loop will continue until the condition is false:

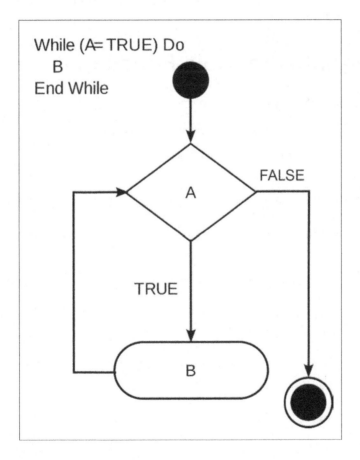

Here's a simple example:

```php
<?php
    $count = 1;

    while($count < 25){
        echo "Count: " . $count . "\n";

        $count += 1;
}

?>
```

We take the preceding count variable and assign it the value of 1. The while condition checks to see whether the count variable is less than 25, and will break once the counter variable equals 25. Inside of the while function, we echo out the current count, and then increment the count variable by 1.

Working with the while Function

In this section, we will build a while function which will iterate while the counter is less than 30. Follow these steps::

1. Open your code editor and create a new file, while.php.

2. Within the new file, create your open and close php tags:

   ```php
   <?php

   ?>
   ```

3. Next, we define a counter function and initialize it with the number 1:

   ```php
   <?php
   $count = 1;
   ?>
   ```

4. Then, we can create a while loop that will echo out the current count, and then increase counter by 1:

   ```php
   <?php

           $count = 1;

           while($count <= 30){
   ```

```
        echo "Count " . $count . "\n";
        $count++;
    }
?>
```

5. Open your working directory in the Terminal, and type the following command:

```
php while.php
```

Do-While Loops

Do-while loops are just like while loops, but instead of running the condition at the beginning of the loop, they check after the internal code block has been run. The idea is that if you need the block of code to run at least once, you use this loop instead of a while loop.

 Do-while loops are also called exit controlled loops.

Do-while loops are represented as follows:

```
<?php

    do{

}while(condition);

?>
```

We are going to modify the while loop from what precedes:

```
<?php
    $count = 1;

    do{
        echo "Count: " . $count . "\n";


        $count++;

}while($count <= 25);
?>
```

Conversion of a while Loop to a do-while Loop

In this section, we are going to copy the previous example, but convert the while loop to a do-while loop so that you can see the differences in how they function. Follow these steps:

1. Create a new file and call it `dowhile.php`.

2. Next, open up the `while.php` file and copy the contents into the `dowhile.php` file.

3. We are now going to modify the `while` function to resemble the following code:

```php
<?php

        $count = 1;

        do{
            echo "Count " . $count . "\n";
            $count++;
        }while($count <= 30);
?>
```

4. Open your working directory in the Terminal, and type the following command:

```
php dowhile.php
```

foreach Loops

foreach loops are next on our list. foreach loops are designed to give programmers a simple way to iterate through an array. This loop will only work with arrays and objects, which you will learn about later in this book. There are two syntaxes for this loop:

```php
<?php

    foreach($array as $value){

    }

?>
```

The first syntax takes a given array and iterates through each element in the array, assigning it to the secondary variable. For example:

```php
<?php
        $students = array("Jill", "John", "Tom", "Amy");

        foreach($students as $student){
            echo $student . "\n";
}
?>
```

In the preceding example, we define an array filled with students' names. We then use the foreach loop to iterate through our students array and echo out each name.

The second syntax is written as follows:

```php
<?php
    foreach($array as $key => $value){

}
?>
```

In this version of the for each function, the given array is iterated through, but instead of giving a single element, it gives you both the key and the element itself. Here's an example of how we'll use it:

 For the full code snippet, refer to the Lesson 2.php file in the code files folder.

```php
<?php

    $students = array(
    "Jill" => array(
    "age" => 20,
    "favorite_color" => "blue"
),
.....
);

    foreach($students as $name => $info){
    echo $name . "'s is " . $info['age'] . " years old\n";
}
?>
```

In this example, we define a multidimensional array that stores each student's age and favorite color and is indexed using the student's name. We then use the `foreach` function to iterate through the `students` array and assign each element's key to the `name` variable and the student's info to the `info` variable. Within the loop, we `echo` out the student's name, along with their age.

Activity: Working with the foreach Loop

Let's put our understanding of for each loops into practice.

Your manager has asked you to create a PHP script that will calculate how much each employee makes per month, based on their given salary.

This is what you do:

1. Create a new directory and name it `monthly_payment`.

2. Within the new directory, create an `index.php` file.

3. First, you'll define the multidimensional array that will store the employee's name, job title, and salary:

    ```php
    <?php

    $employees = array(
        array(
            "name" => "John Doe",
            "title" => "Programmer",
            "salary" => 60000
    ....
            "title" => "Manager",
            "salary" => 132000
        )
    );
    ?>
    ```

4. Next, define the `foreach` loop that will iterate through the `employee` array:

    ```php
    foreach($employees as $employee){
    }
    ```

5. Finally, add an `echo` statement that will print the name, title, and calculated monthly pay:

```
foreach($employees as $employee){
    echo $employee['name'] . "(" . $employee['title'] . ") annual
salary is $" .
    $employee['salary'] . " and earns $" . ($employee['salary'] /
12) . "/mo. \n";
        }
```

The calculator script is now done. If you need to add additional employees, it is as easy as adding an additional associative array with the employee's info.

Summary

We have reached the end of the second chapter. In this chapter, we have seen how to declare and define an array and have covered the different types of arrays. We saw the various operations that can be performed on an array. We have also covered control flow statements such as the for loop, while loop, and do while loop.

In the next chapter, we are going to learn about code reusability using functions and classes, taking you one step closer to building your own custom application.

3

Functions and Classes

In the previous chapter, we saw how to declare and define an array and covered multiple types of arrays such as the indexed array, associative arrays, and so on. We also saw the various operations that can be performed on an array.

In this chapter, we will identify how to define and call functions. We will also learn how to create classes, and how to use the classes and functions together.

Functions are blocks of code that are packaged into reusable code. A function is a piece of code that returns a value by doing some processing, taking one or more outputs.

A class is a blueprint for an object. Classes form the structure of data and the actions that utilize the information to create objects.

By the end of this chapter, you will be able to:

- Define and call functions
- Define classes and create instances of the class using the `new` keyword
- Implement and call `public` and `static` class functions

Functions

Functions are like a machine with a fix defined logic. On one end, it takes a parameter, processes it, and returns a value based on the input and function definition.

Functions are used to reuse a particular block of code again and again instead of defining it when needed all the time:

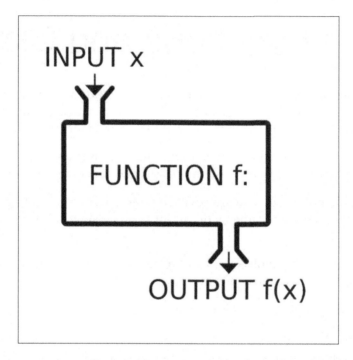

To define a function, we use the keyword `function`, followed by the name that we want to give the function; and, within curly brackets, we define the operation of the function. For example, if we want to create a function to print out, "Hello World," we write the following:

```php
<?php
    function HelloWorld(){
        echo "Hello World";
    }
?>
```

If we were to write this function in a new file and run it, it wouldn't display anything, and that's because we haven't called the function; we have only defined it.

To call the function, we add the following line of code:

```php
<?php
HelloWorld();
?>
```

When creating functions, you sometimes need to have additional parameters passed to your function; this can be done when defining your new function.

Let's modify the previous example to accept a name parameter:

```php
<?php
    function HelloWorld($name){
        echo "Hello World, " . $name;
}
?>
```

To pass the name, we define a variable within the parentheses following the function name.

Now, when we call the function, we can pass whatever value we want through that variable, and it will be printed out:

```php
<?php
    HelloWorld("John");
?>
```

Sometimes, when we create a function, we know that there will be cases where we won't pass a value. In those cases, we will want a default value to be passed automatically.

To set a default value, you should assign it to the specified variable when you set it, as shown here:

```php
<?php
    function displayMessage($message = "World"){
        echo "Hello " . $message;
}
displayMessage();
displayMessage("Greg");
?>
```

Functions can be used not only to print messages to the screen but also to return a value back, which can be stored in a variable or used in another function. For example, if you create an addition function, you might want to return the sum:

```php
<?php
    function addNumbers($a, $b){
        return $a + $b;
    }
}
echo addNumbers(5,6);
?>
```

Now that we have a function that can return a value, let's see how to use it to store a value:

```php
<?php
    $sum = addNumbers(1,2);
?>
```

 In your program, you may sometimes need to dynamically call a function with efficiency. PHP gives you a helpful tool to do just that - `call_user_func_array`. The `call_user_func_array` function allows you to call a function by passing its name as the first parameter, and provide arguments as an array through the second parameter.

Creating a Simple Function

In this section, we are going to create a simple function that will calculate the discount of a given percentage. To do this, follow these steps:

1. Open your code editor and create a new file, `function.php`.

2. Within the new file, create your open and close php tags:

    ```php
    <?php

    ?>
    ```

3. Now, we are going to create two new variables: `$sweaterPrice` and `$precentOff`. They will store the original price of the product, as well as the percent off:

```php
<?php
$sweaterPrice = 50;
$percentOff = 0.25;
?>
```

4. Now that we have our variables, we can define our function. Our function is simple; it accepts a price and discount percentage. Inside of the function, we multiply the price by the discount percentage and return the product:

```php
<?php
    $sweaterPrice = 50;
    $percentOff = 0.25;

    function couponCode($price, $discount){
        return $price * $discount;
    }
?>
```

5. Finally, we can go ahead and print our message about the discount to our users, using our newly created function:

```php
<?php

    $sweaterPrice = 50;
    $percentOff = 0.25;

    function couponCode($price, $discount){
        return $price * $discount;
    }
    echo "The sweater originally costs $" . $sweaterPrice
. " with the discount you'll pay $" . ($sweaterPrice -
couponCode($sweaterPrice, $percentOff)) . "\n";
?>
```

Now that you have an understanding of functions, you should be comfortable with developing reusable code and applying them. In the next section, we will learn about classes. Classes will give us a better understanding of structuring code and properties into a neat package.

Classes

In this section, you are going to learn about classes. Classes fall into a type of programming called object-oriented programming, which simply means organizing your code into what is known as an object. Objects allow you to create a base package that has its own variables and methods, exclusive to the object.

 Think of a class as a blueprint for an object. There is only one class, but you can have many instantiations. This can be compared to the blueprint for a house. Many new homes can be built from the same blueprint.

Let's suppose that we want to create a class that holds our student's information. We would define it as follows:

```php
<?php

    class Student {

    }

?>
```

This is the basic student class, in its simplest form. We start by using the keyword class, followed by the name of our class, which, in this case, is Student. Next, we create a code block with open and close parentheses. Within the open and close parenthesis, we add the contents of our class.

This leads to the next section for classes: member variables. We worked with variables in *Chapter 1, Getting Started with PHP,* of this book. As a refresher, variables act as a container that allows you to store data temporarily. Member variables have the same function, but are scoped within the boundaries of a given class or class instance.

We will extend our Student class to store the student's name, age, and major:

```php
<?php

    class Student {
        public $name;
```

```
        public $age;
        public $major;
    }

?>
```

You should notice the `public` keyword that we use when defining our variables. This is important, as it tells the program how the data can be accessed. The `public` keyword simply states that you can access this data directly.

Now that we have our class ready, we can create a new instance of the class and assign it to a variable that we can use to interact with the class's properties:

```php
<?php

    $michael = new Student();

    $michael->name = "Michael John";
    $michael->age = 27;
    $michael->major = "Computer Science";
?>
```

In this example, we create a new instance of the student class by using the `new` keyword and assign it to a variable that we call `Michael`. Then, using the arrow syntax, we can access the public values to set the name, age, and major.

With classes, we sometimes have cases where we want to instantiate a new instance of a class with values. We can do this with a function called a constructor:

```
public function __construct(){

}
```

This function is the default function that is called when you use the `new` keyword to instantiate a new class. For passing values, we would define the values within the construct function.

For example, if we want to set the student's info, we do the following:

```php
<?php

class Student {
    public $name;
    public $age;
    public $major;
```

```php
        public function __construct($name, $age, $major){
            $this->name = $name;
            $this->age = $age;
            $this->major = $major;
        }
    }

?>
```

Now, we can provide the student's info:

```php
<?php
    $michael = new Student("Michael John", 27, "Computer
Science");
?>
```

Along with the public variables, you can also define private variables. The private keyword makes variables accessible only by methods themselves. This means that the only time that you can access those types of variables is through the constructor, getter functions, and setter functions, which gives us a great insight into class functions.

Class functions allow you to create local functionality for a class to set, get, and mutate the data held within the class itself. For example, if we take our previous class definition and replace the public variables with private variables, it will look as follows:

```php
<?php

    class Student {
        private $name;
        private $age;
        private $major;

        public function __construct($name, $age, $major){
            $this->name = $name;
            $this->age = $age;
            $this->major = $major;
        }
    }

?>
```

What if we want to change these values, or to put these values somewhere else in the program? We define functions, of course:

 For the full code snippet, refer to the Lesson 3.php file in the code files folder.

```php
<?php

    class Student {
        private $name;
        private $age;
        private $major;
. . . .
        }
public function getName(){
            return $this->name;
    }
}

public function getAge(){
    return $this->age;
}
public function getMajor(){
    return $this->major;
}
    }

?>
```

Keep in mind that using set and get in the name of the function isn't required; you can use whatever name you want to - something that allows you to easily remember what each function does. As you can see in the code example, you can update the private values using the respective set functions, and retrieve those values using the respective get functions.

For example, suppose that Michael changed his major:

```php
<?php

    ...

    $michael->setMajor("Engineering");

?>
```

If we want to see what his major is, we can use the following code:

```php
<?php

    echo "Michael's major is " . $michael->getMajor();

?>
```

Classes are a very powerful tool when it comes to any type of programming, mainly due to the idea of inheritance. Inheritance allows you to create a base class that defines general functions and variables and will be used by all of the children of the class.

For a simple example, let's define an Animal class:

```php
<?php

    class Animal{
        public $sound;
        public $name;

        public function speak(){
            echo $this->name . " says " . $this->sound;
        }
    }

?>
```

This base class has a variable that holds the animal name and the sound that the animal makes. Additionally, it has a public function, speak, that will print the sound that the animal makes.

We can extend different types of animals from the base class.

Let's suppose that we want to define a Dog class:

```php
<?php
    class Dog extends Animal {
        public $name = "Dog";
        public $sound = "Woof! Woof!";
}

?>
```

We simply change the value of the name and sound variables, and we have our dog class:

```php
<?php

    $dog = new Dog();

    $dog->speak();

?>
```

When developing child classes, one thing to keep in mind is that you can extend the base constructor by doing the following:

```php
<?php
    class Dog extends Animal {
        public $name = "Dog";
        public $sound = "Woof! Woof!";

        public function __construct(){
            parent::__construct();
        }
}

?>
```

Another useful section, when it comes to classes, are static functions. Static functions don't require that an instance of a class is created in order to be used. This comes in handy when you build a class to house utility functions. To create a static function, you simply use the static keyword:

```php
<?php

    class Animal{
        public $sound;
        public $name;
```

```php
public function speak(){
        echo $this->name . " says " . $this->sound;
    }

    public static function about(){
        echo "This is the animal base class.";
    }
}

?>
```

In the preceding example, we create a static about function that will give a little description of the class, when called. You can use this function as follows:

```php
<?php
    echo Animal::about();
?>
```

Activity: Calculate the Monthly Pay of an Employee

You have been assigned to calculate the monthly pay of an employee. The salary should be calculated and displayed on the screen.

The aim of this activity is for you to learn how to calculate the discount from a given percentage.

Follow these steps to perform this activity:

1. Open your code editor and create a new file, class.php.

2. Within the new file, create your open and close php tags:

    ```php
    <?php

    ?>
    ```

3. Next, define a base employee class:

 For the full code snippet, refer to the Lesson 3.php file in the code files folder.

```php
<?php

    class BaseEmployee {
        private $name;
        private $title;
        private $salary;

        function __construct($name, $title, $salary){
            $this->name = $name;
            $this->title = $title;
            $this->salary = $salary;
    }

        public function setName($name){
            $this->name = $name;
. . . . . .
        }
        public function getTitle(){
            return $this->title;
        }

        public function getSalary(){
            return $this->salary;
        }
    }

?>
```

4. From this base class, we can go ahead and create an `employee` class that extends the base class. In this extended class, we will add an additional function, which will calculate the monthly pay of an employee:

 For the full code snippet, refer to the `Lesson 3.php` file in the code files folder.

```php
<?php
    class BaseEmployee {
        private $name;
        private $title;
        private $salary;

        function __construct($name, $title, $salary){
...

        public function getSalary(){
        return $this->salary;
        }
    }

    class Employee extends BaseEmployee{
        public function calculateMonthlyPay(){
            return $this->salary / 12;
        }
    }
?>
```

5. Lastly, we will use the new class to print the monthly pay:

 For the full code snippet, refer to the Lesson 3.php file in the code files folder.

```php
<?php

    class BaseEmployee {
        private $name;
        private $title;
        private $salary;
......
    class Employee extends BaseEmployee{
        public function calculateMonthlyPay(){
            return $this->salary / 12;
        }
    }


    $markus = new Employee("Markus Gray", "CEO", 100000);

    echo "Monthly Pay is " . $markus->calculateMonthlyPay();

?>
```

Summary

In this chapter, we learned about functions and classes. We covered how to define and call functions. We also covered how to define classes and use classes and functions together. As we begin to build larger and more complex projects, functions and classes will help us to create highly organized code and maintain best practices.

In the next chapter, we will cover data operations like input and output data, catching and handling errors using error handling, and we will also cover the basics of MySQL.

4
Data Operations

In the previous chapter, we learned about functions and classes. We covered how to define and call functions. We also covered how to define classes and use classes and functions together.

In this chapter, we will focus on handling input from users and printing outcomes back to them, handling errors gracefully, and learning the basics of using the MySQL database.

By the end of this chapter, you will be able to:

- Identify how to accept input from the user and print it to the screen
- Implement the basics of using MySQL

Inputting and Outputting Data

Being able to accept input from a user is a major requirement when moving from building websites with PHP to building web applications with PHP. Typically, input comes from HTML forms.

Let's create a simple contact form:

```html
<html>
<body>
    <form action="index.php" method="POST">
        <input type="text" name="name" />
        <input type="text" name="email" />
        <textarea name="message"></textarea>
        <button type="submit">Send</button>
    </form>
</body>
</html>
```

In the preceding contact form, we see input for a user's name, email, and a message. The method that we are going to use to submit this form is called a POST request.

To read the data that is being submitted, we are going to add some PHP to the top of the form, which will read and render data from our POST request:

 For the full code snippet, refer to the Lesson 4.php file in the code files folder.

```php
<?php
    if($_POST){
        echo "Name: " . $_POST['name'] . "\n";
        echo "Email: " . $_POST['email'] . "\n";
......
        <input type="text" name="email" />
        <textarea name="message"></textarea>
        <button type="submit">Send</button>
    </form>
</body>
</html>
```

As you can see, it's easy to accept input from our application's user. In the preceding code example, we use a special variable, $_POST array, to access all of the data that is submitted via a POST request. The $_POST variable, an associative array, and the content can be accessed via the names you specify in the input elements.

Another request type that you can use is GET request. GET requests are used more often than you might think; GET is the request type that you use when you navigate to a website or perform a search on Google. The input for a GET request is done via a query string.

A query string is a string that is attached to the end of a URL, prepended with a question mark, as seen here: `https://www.example.com?name=Michael&age=12`:

In the preceding example, you can see that we have two keys that are separated with an ampersand. Just like in the POST method, there is a special variable for a GET request, and that is the $_GET variable (which is an associative array, as well).

If we want to get the name from the previous query string, you can use this line of code:

```php
<?php

    $name = $_GET['name'];

?>
```

You can use the GET request with the form, as well. Let's revisit the form element that we saw before:

For the full code snippet, refer to the Lesson 4.php file in the code files folder.

```php
<?php
    if($_GET){
        echo "Name: " . $_GET['name'] . "\n";
        echo "Email: " . $_GET['email'] . "\n";
......
        <button type="submit">Send</button>
    </form>
</body>
</html>
```

In the form's method attribute, we changed it to GET, swapping the $_POST variable with the $_GET variable.

When accepting user input, it's sometimes necessary to clean up the input before doing anything with it. Some input requires cleaning any whitespace from the beginning and end. This is where PHP's trim function comes in to play. The trim function will clean whitespace, and other similar characters, from both sides of the user's input. If you want to remove from either the left or right side, you can use the ltrim and rtrim functions, respectively.

Building a Form for Our User List

We are going to start off by building a form for our user list. At the end of this section, you will have a form that will accept your firstname, lastname, and email. It will have a submit button at the end, to submit the information:

1. Create a new directory and call it users_list.

2. In the new directory, create an index.php file.

3. Open the index.php file in your text editor, and add the form code:

For the full code snippet, refer to the Lesson 4.php file in the code files folder.

```
<html>
    <body>
        <form action="index.php" method="post">
. . . . . .
        </form>
    </body>
</html>
```

4. Now that we have our form, we want to be able to view the data submitted to the form:

For the full code snippet, refer to the Lesson 4.php file in the code files folder.

```php
<?php
    if($_POST){
        echo "First Name: " . $_POST['firstname'] . "\n";
        echo "Last Name: " . $_POST['lastname'] . "\n";
. . . . . .
id="email"/>
            <br>
            <button type="submit">Save</button>
        </form>
    </body>
</html>
```

5. Now, to see our form in action, we will open the working directory in the Terminal and run the following command:

```
php -S localhost:8000 -t
```

With any web application, you are going to need to have a way to store data. The service that permits you to persist your current state in MySQL database is known as persistence. If variables allow you to store data temporarily, persistence allows you to store the data in databases long term.

The primary database type that is used in PHP is MySQL. MySQL databases are known as relational-based databases that are organized into tables.

In this section, we will cover how to use a MySQL database with PHP, and how to perform various operations with it.

Connect to a Database

The first step for using a database is to connect to one. In this chapter, we are going to focus on using the PDO, or PHP Data Object, style of usage.

To connect to a database, use the following lines of code:

For the full code snippet, refer to the Lesson 4.php file in the code files folder.

MySQL Basics

```php
<?php
    $host = "DATABASE_HOST";
    $username = "DATABASE_USERNAME";
    $password = "DATABASE_PASSWORD";
    $database = "DATABASE_NAME";
......

            echo "Connected successfully";
        }
    catch(PDOException $e)
        {

            echo "Connection failed: " . $e->getMessage();
    }
?>
```

In the preceding code, you can see that we have a good chunk of new code. We start off by defining four new variables to hold the credential values for our database: one for the host URL, one for the username, one for the password, and finally, one for the name of the database that we are connecting to. Next, we wrap the database connection code within a try block; this will catch any errors that come up when we connect to the database and run queries. Within the try block, we initiate a new instance of the PDO class by using the credential variables we defined earlier, assigning it to the $conn variable. We then set the error mode to ensure that it triggers our catch block if any errors occur. Lastly, in the try section, we echo out a successful connection message. In the catch section of the try/catch block, we simply echo out the error message that was triggered.

Create a Database Table

We will now create a table using an SQL query:

 For the full code snippet, refer to the Lesson 4.php file in the code files folder.

```php
<?php
    $host = "DATABASE_HOST";
    $username = "DATABASE_USERNAME";
    $password = "DATABASE_PASSWORD";
......
```

```
    }
    catch(PDOException $e)
    {

        echo "Connection failed: " . $e->getMessage();


    }
    }
?>
```

To create a table, we use the CREATE TABLE command, followed by the name of the table. Then, inside a pair of parentheses, we define the fields for the table. The table that we created in the query will create a user's table, which will hold the user's ID (the primary key of this table) and will auto-increment a user's name of the type varchar, with a maximum of 60 characters. The table will also hold an email address of the type varchar, with a maximum of 30 characters.

Insert a Record into the Database

We now have a table in our database, and we can add data to it. We add data using an insert query. After we connect to the database and set the error mode, we can define our query. The Insert query starts with the INSERT INTO command, followed by the name of the table that we are inserting data into. In a pair of parentheses, we define the fields that we are going to write to. Right after the fields, we define the values that we want to enter into the table:

 For the full code snippet, refer to the Lesson 4.php file in the code files folder.

```
<?php
    $host = "DATABASE_HOST";
    $username = "DATABASE_USERNAME";
    $password = "DATABASE_PASSWORD";
    $database = "DATABASE_NAME";

    try {
        $conn = new PDO("mysql:host=$host;dbname=$database",
$username, $password);


    ......


    }
    catch(PDOException $e)
```

```
    {

        echo "Connection failed: " . $e->getMessage();

    }
?>
```

Fetch a Single Row from a Database Table

If you want to fetch a user from the database, you use a SELECT query. In this case, we want to get the new user that we inserted in the previous code block. We'll use the following code:

 For the full code snippet, refer to the Lesson 4.php file in the code files folder.

```
<?php
    $host = "DATABASE_HOST";
    $username = "DATABASE_USERNAME";
    $password = "DATABASE_PASSWORD";
    $database = "DATABASE_NAME";

    try {
        $conn = new PDO("mysql:host=$host;dbname=$database",
$username, $password);
    ......

    }
    catch(PDOException $e)
    {

        echo "Connection failed: " . $e->getMessage();

    }
?>
```

Using the $conn variable, we prepare a SELECT query, indicating that we want to pull information from the users table; we then use the WHERE clause to define the conditions for the desired information. To finally run the query, we execute the prepared statement, passing an array with the required email address. Since we want to have an associative array returned to us, we set the fetch model to FETCH_ ASSOC, getting the single record by using the fetch method.

To render the user array, we use the PRINT command in between the open and close pre tags.

> pre tags beautifies an array that has been printed. This is typically used to debug what is contained within an array.

Fetch Multiple Rows from a Database Table

If we want to fetch all of the users in a table, we do away with the prepared statements and run a query directly. This time around, we remove the WHERE clause. Instead of using the fetch function, we use the fetch_all function:

> For the full code snippet, refer to the Lesson 4.php file in the code files folder.

```php
<?php
    $host = "DATABASE_HOST";
    $username = "DATABASE_USERNAME";
    $password = "DATABASE_PASSWORD";
    $database = "DATABASE_NAME";

    try {
        $conn = new PDO("mysql:host=$host;dbname=$database",
$username, $password);
......
        echo "</pre>";

    }
<?php
    $host = "DATABASE_HOST";
    $username = "DATABASE_USERNAME";
    $password = "DATABASE_PASSWORD";
```

```
        $database = "DATABASE_NAME";

        try {
            $conn = new PDO("mysql:host=$host;dbname=$database",
    $username, $password);
    ......
            echo "</pre>";

        }
        catch(PDOException $e)
        {

            echo "Connection failed: " . $e->getMessage();

        }
    ?>
```

Update a Record in a Database Table

Now that we understand how to add and fetch data from a database table, we can start to edit individual records. In MySQL, we update data by using an UPDATE query. To run an UPDATE query, we go back to our prepared statements and start our query with the command UPDATE, followed by the name of the table (in this case, the users table). Next, we use the SET command to start the process of defining the fields and the values that need to be updated, and then we add a WHERE clause to isolate the specific record(s) that we want to have the new values. To add a bit of feedback to how the query went, echo out the count via the row count function.

Let's change our user's email address to test123@email.com:

For the full code snippet, refer to the Lesson 4.php file in the code files folder.

```php
<?php
    $host = "DATABASE_HOST";
    $username = "DATABASE_USERNAME";
    $password = "DATABASE_PASSWORD";
```

```php
    $database = "DATABASE_NAME";

    try {
        $conn = new PDO("mysql:host=$host;dbname=$database",
$username, $password);
......
            echo $statement->rowCount() . "(s) rows affected.";
    }
    catch(PDOException $e)
    {

        echo "Connection failed: " . $e->getMessage();

    }
?>
```

Delete a Record in a Database Table

Our final section in MySQL will be removing data from a database. To remove data, we use the DELETE query. The DELETE query starts with DELETE FROM, followed by the name of the table you are looking to remove data from; finish the query with a WHERE clause, to further specify the record you wish to delete. We place this query in a prepared statement, then execute it by passing the value of the WHERE clause:

 For the full code snippet, refer to the Lesson 4.php file in the code files folder.

```php
<?php
    $host = "DATABASE_HOST";
    $username = "DATABASE_USERNAME";
    $password = "DATABASE_PASSWORD";
    $database = "DATABASE_NAME";

    try {
        $conn = new PDO("mysql:host=$host;dbname=$database",
$username, $password);
......
            echo $statement->rowCount() . "(s) rows deleted.";
```

```
    }
    catch(PDOException $e)
    {
        echo "Connection failed: " . $e->getMessage();

    }
?>
```

Creating an employee Table

Our final project will be to store the input that we get from the users within a database table. Before we get into writing the code to add the data to the database, we need to create a database, as follows:

1. Open the Terminal.

2. Connect to MySQL using the following command:

   ```
   mysql -u root -p
   ```

3. Next, create the `packt_database` database:

   ```
   create database packt_database;
   ```

4. Tell MySQL to use the newly created database:

   ```
   use packt_database;
   ```

5. Finally, create the users table:

   ```
   CREATE TABLE users (
               id INT(6) UNSIGNED AUTO_INCREMENT PRIMARY,
               firstname VARCHAR(30) NOT NULL,
              lastname VARCHAR(30) NOT NULL,
   email VARCHAR(30) NOT NULL
   );
   ```

6. Now, we can close our Terminal and get started finishing our app.

Adding Users to a Database

In this section, we are going to add users to our database using PHP. We then create a form where we accept the INSERT query from the user.

To perform this, perform these steps:

1. Reopen the `users_list` directory in your text editor.

2. Within the second `if` statement, connect to your database:

 For the full code snippet, refer to the `Lesson 4.php` file in the code files folder.

```php
<?php

    if($_POST){
        if(!$_POST['firstname'] || !$_POST['lastname'] || !$_
POST['email']){
            exit("All fields are required.");
        }

        $host = "DATABASE_HOST";
        $username = "DATABASE_USERNAME";
        $password = "DATABASE_PASSWORD";
        $database = "packt_database";

        try {
            $conn = new PDO("mysql:host=$host;dbname=$database",
$username, $password);
......
    <button type="submit">Save</button>
        </form>
    </body>
</html>
```

3. Next, go ahead and use an `INSERT` query to add the input that you receive from the user to the database:

 For the full code snippet, refer to the `Lesson 4.php` file in the code files folder.

```php
<?php

    if($_POST){
        if(!$_POST['firstname'] || !$_POST['lastname'] || !$_
POST['email']){
            exit("All fields are required.");
        }

.......

            <br>
            <label>Email</label>
            <input type="text" name="email" id="email"/>
            <br>
            <button type="submit">Save</button>
        </form>
    </body>
</html>
```

4. Now, you're ready to test out the simple app. Open the user_list directory in the Terminal and use the following command to serve your app:

```
php -S localhost:8000 -t .
```

Summary

We have reached the end of this chapter. In this chapter, we learned how to accept a user's input, and how to access it via PHP. Finally, we learned the basics of using MySQL databases, and applied all of the principles into a mini app that adds users to a database via a web form.

In the next chapter, we will cover the basics of building a PHP web application using Object Oriented Programming principles such as namespaces, use statements, access modifiers, and so on. We will also cover how to structure an application properly using MVC design concepts.

5
Building a PHP Web Application

In the previous chapter, we learned how to accept a user's input, and how to access it via PHP. We also learned the basics of using MySQL databases, and applied all of the principles of the previous chapters into a mini app that adds users to a database via a web form.

In this chapter, we will be learning and applying OOP concepts in a framework. We will cover error reporting using the Whoops library and will learn how to handle those errors. We will also cover how to manage and structure our application in a framework.

By the end of this chapter, you will be able to:

- Apply OOP concepts in a framework environment
- Structure files and folders to make a framework
- Describe how a framework interacts with a data source
- Build a framework using the MVC design pattern
- Build a CRM application to manage contacts on your framework

Building an application will require us to know about the underlying framework and how we can create the application using the MVC architecture style of building. A PHP framework is a collection of folders and files designed to promote code reuse organization; the folders and files provide a common code base to build applications on top of. Through these chapters, you will learn how to build such a framework.

A common design pattern that we will use throughout this book is called CRUD - an acronym that means:

- **Create**: Creating a new MySQL record
- **Read**: Reading records from a database
- **Update**: Updating a MySQL record
- **Delete:** Deleting a MySQL record

CRUD sits at the heart of any practical application that is built in a framework. Almost everything can be broken down into CRUD.

An example of CRUD would involve creating new content, reading the content, and having prompts to update and delete the content.

We will be using a design pattern known as Model View Controller (MVC), which is a way to structure the directories and files upon which your framework is based. Structuring and examples will be shown using an MVC structure:

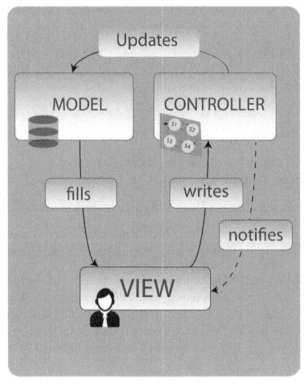

A representation of Model View Controller (MVC)

PHP Standard Recommendation (PSR) sets a style guide for formatting your code, allowing for maximum compatibility with other code that you may come into contact with: `http://www.php-fig.org/psr/`.

Concepts of OOP in a Framework Environment

It is a good idea to have a solid understanding of PHP object-oriented programming (OOP) concepts before starting to learn how a framework is constructed. One thing that all PHP frameworks have in common is that they are first and foremost built on top of OOP PHP; essentially, they are just a way to organize your files.

We will learn about the following OOP concepts:

- Namespaces
- Use Statements
- Classes and Objects
- Methods
- Access Modifiers

Namespaces

Namespacing can be compared to a folder structure. The primary purpose of a namespace is to allow classes to have the same name, but under different namespaces.

Namespacing is case-sensitive. A namespace should start with a capital letter and use camel case thereafter - the beginning of each word should start off lowercase, with each subsequent word in uppercase.

For example: `mySpace`

An example of this would be if you had a class called `Post` and, in another folder, you had a class called `Post`. Normally, you would not be able to use these in the same file, as the classes would conflict with each other; however, if each of the classes has a namespace of the folder in which they are stored, then you can use them in the same file.

The file file1.txt can exist in both the directory `/home/packt` and in `/home/other`, but two copies of file1.txt cannot co-exist in the same directory. In addition, to access `file1.txt` outside of the `/home/packt` directory, we must prepend the directory name to the filename, using the directory separator to get `/home/packt/file1.txt`. This same principle extends to namespaces in the programming world.

You cannot use two classes within the same file, as they will conflict with each other. To get around this, you can give one of the classes an alias. Think of an alias as a nickname for that class.

A namespace is making a reference to the location within the file structure in the `app/controllers` directory: the namespace `App\Controllers` is the path to its location. Notice the use of the backslash character when writing a namespace:

```
//valid namespace
namespace App\Controllers;
```

Namespace App, Controllers, and Use Statements

Use statements are a way to import a class, rather than having to manually include them in. use statements are used in conjunction with composer.

As an example of using a use statement in a class, if we want to use a `Contact` model, we can place the following code at the top of the class:

```
use App\Models\Contact;
```

When you have a class called `Contact` that has a namespace of `App\Models`, to import it, you can use `App\Models\Contact`. You can then refer to this class by calling `Contact`; you don't have to refer to its full namespace, as it's already been imported:

[

We use composer for auto-loading filesbasedontheirnamespaces, and we will cover this in detail in a later chapter.
]

```
//start with the namespace
namespace App\Controllers;
//add the use statement
use App\Models\Contact;
//make the call
$contact = new Contact();
```

Defining Classes and Objects Using Namespaces

We learned how to create classes and objects in the previous chapter. We will now see how to create classes and objects using namespaces.

An object is a class that has been instantiated; for instance, if you look at the last line of the last example, a class called `contact` has been instantiated by using the new operator, followed by the class name. This has created a new object; what this means is that the new object has access to all of the methods of the class and public properties:

```
//start with the namespace
namespace App\Controllers;

//add the use statement
use App\Models\Contact;

//make the call
$contact = new Contact();

//make a call to a getContacts method that exists within the contact
class
$contact->getContacts();
```

Methods

A method is a function that resides inside of a class. In reality, the only difference between a method and a function is the naming convention, and that a method happens to live inside of a class.

Methods are used to retrieve and pass information to or from a class, and to the file where the class is being instantiated:

```
//start with a namespace
namespace App\Models;

//here is an example of a method being defined, in the previous
example the method was being called.
class Contact
{
    public function getContacts()
```

```
    {
                        //get data here
    }
}
```

Access Modifiers

Access modifiers are a way to grant and restrict access to the properties and methods of a class. There are three access modifiers: public, protected, and private. These can be compared to gatekeepers, letting data in or preventing data from entering:

- **Public**

  Defining a property or method as public means that the class, the extended class, and the file where a class is instantiated all have access to read and write the method or property.

- **Protected**

  A protected method or property can only be accessed by the class, or an extended class.

- **Private**

  A private property or method can only be accessed from within the class where it is defined.

 A private property cannot be accessed from outside of that class, and it cannot be accessed from an extended class.

The following are examples of how to make use of the various access modifiers. You will see the public, protected, and private properties in use when defining a property named $token:

```
public $token;
protected $token;
private $token;
```

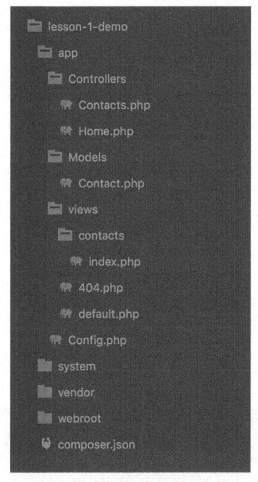

Folder Structure

Explanation:

What we have here is the file structure of the framework that we will be building over the next few chapters:

- The **app** folder is where your application will be held. The **app** holds your controllers, your models, and your views. As mentioned previously, this is part of the MVC structure.

- The **config** file is where the site name and database credentials are stored.

- The **system** folder holds the core files of the framework.

- The **vendor** directory is a composer directory, containing any third-party packages installed via composer. It also stores composer itself.

- The **webroot** folder is your document root; this is what your browser reads from.

Later in this chapter, we will be covering a design pattern named MVC.

The following example uses this design pattern, which is simply a way of organizing your file structure.

In this example, we will pass the details of a single contact from a class that has been instantiated, and display them in a browser.

For now, notice how each of the OOP principles is employed in each file, and see what you recognize.

This code will not work as vanilla PHP, as the structure of a framework is required. This book will teach you how (and why) these components work together the way that they do. The purpose of showing this example is to see OOP concepts in action in a framework setting.

The following is an example of a controller:

```php
Contacts.php                    ×
<?php namespace App\Controllers;

use System\BaseController;
use App\Models\Contact;

class Contacts extends BaseController
{
    public function index()
    {
        //instantiate Contact model
        $contact = new Contact();

        //call the getContacts method and store to a local variable
        $contacts = $contact->getContacts();

        //load a view and pass in the contacts using a compact()
        echo $this->view->render('contacts/index', compact('contacts'));
    }
}
```

Contacts Controller

First, there is a `namespace`, which is how composer knows to load the file. Without composer, a manual include would be required, using an `include` or `require` known as lazy loading, to prevent irrelevant files from being loaded and improve performance.

Following the `namespace` and `use` statements is the class definition (the blueprint of the class). Here, we are naming the class `Contacts`, and we are extending the functionality that is already present is the `BaseController` class:

```php
Contact.php                    ×
<?php
namespace App\Models;

class Contact
{
    public function getContacts()
    {
        //return an array of contacts
        return ['joe', 'bob', 'kerry', 'dave'];
    }
}
```

Contacts Model

Explanation:

The file seen here is the model; the `Contact` model was instantiated in the previous example.

Again, the model contains a `namespace`.

No `use` statement is required, as in this example, the data is contained within the class definition.

If the data was stored in a database or another data source, then the class would need to extend the `BaseModel`:

```
index.php                      ×

<h1>Contacts</h1>

<?php
if ($contacts) {
    foreach($contacts as $contact) {
        echo $contact.'<br>';
    }
}
?>
```

Contact View

Minimal PHP is used in the view; data is usually passed to a view in an array or a variable, and styling is dictated:

Browser View

In your early years as a developer, you may find that you frequently forget to use a semicolon; in fact, David, one of our book creators, frequently recalls how he once spent nearly two whole days trying to resolve a bug in one of this first projects, only to find that the problem was a missing semicolon.

When working in a framework environment, forgetting to use the right case can be a lot like forgetting to use the semicolon.

 This does not need to be the case; you can make use of software specialist add-ons, known as PHP linters, that will check for problems like forgetting to use the correct case. PHP linters highlight the code before you run the script. You will find such add-ons in IDEs such as PHP Storm, or in text editors like Sublime Text or Atom:

- `https://www.jetbrains.com/phpstorm/` made by Jet Brains
- `https://www.sublimetext.com/` made by Sublime HQ
- `https://atom.io/` made by Atom

Structure of a Framework

At its core, MVC is a separation of concerns, so all data sources come from the model or a database resource. Your controller controls the flow of the application and resides in a controllers directory. All of the markup lives inside what is known as the view. Together, they form the Model View Controller (MVC) design pattern.

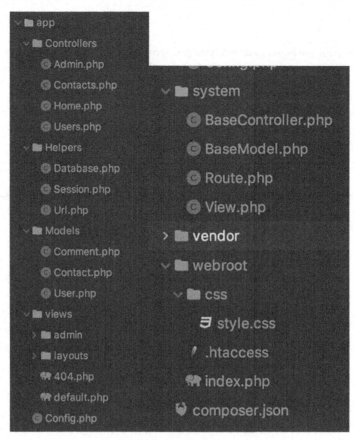

Framework Folder and File Structure

If you need to modify a data source, you know to go to the model to do it; if you want to change how it looks, you know to go to the view; and to change the control of the application, you go to the controller.

> Note that the model is not restricted to pulling data from a database; this is a common misconception. Our earlier example highlights this.

Other sources of data in a model could be static data or data read from a file or an external feed like an RSS.

Explanation:

When working with a framework, much of your application will be built using the MVC design pattern.

Both a model and a controller will extend functionality from the `BaseModel` and `BaseController` stored in the system directory. You will likely not need to change these frequently. Any application that is built on top of the framework will be largely contained in the model, controllers, and views directories that are stored in the `App` directory:

```php
Contacts.php                    ×
<?php namespace App\Controllers;

use System\BaseController;
use App\Models\Contact;

class Contacts extends BaseController
{
    public function index()
    {
        //instantiate Contact model
        $contact = new Contact();

        //call the getContacts method and store to a local variable
        $contacts = $contact->getContacts();

        //load a view and pass in the contacts using a compact()
        echo $this->view->render('contacts/index', compact('contacts'));
    }
}
```

Contacts Controller

Here, the controller is communicating with the model. The model is providing the controller with a source of data. The controller is the brain of the structure, and here, it is a series of instructions for when to serve the data source and how to behave under what conditions.

The contact class has a function that will be called when the user visits a certain URI (how this works, and why this works, will be covered in later chapters); this initiates contact with the model.

In this example, the controller is not concerned with what is contained in the data source; however, it can be programmed to examine this data.

After the data is obtained by the controller, it is stored and passed to the view:

```php
Contact.php                    ×
<?php
namespace App\Models;

class Contact
{
    public function getContacts()
    {
        //return an array of contacts
        return ['joe', 'bob', 'kerry', 'dave'];
    }
}
```

Contacts Model

Explanation:

The contacts model has a data source that contains the knowledge of an application, but on its own, it cannot make use of this knowledge. It can only give instructions to manage the knowledge. The CRUD principle comes into play in a model, where there are methods to create, read, update, and delete from the Model's source of knowledge.

In this case, the data source is an array of names:

```
index.php                    ×

<h1>Contacts</h1>

<?php
if ($contacts) {
    foreach($contacts as $contact) {
        echo $contact.'<br>';
    }
}
?>
```

Contact View

In the view file, you will see that the data is taken as it is served; in this case, the view is served an array of names. These names are thorough, and displayed with any markup and styling applied.

In a framework, the view is part of a wider structure that applies global elements such as headers and footers in your web applications, as well as CSS and JavaScript files.

It is possible to loop through an array, but all processing should be completed in the controller, when possible.

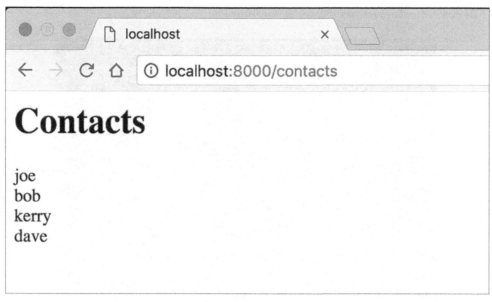

Browser View

You have now identified how OOP principles can be used in an MVC framework example.

Now, let's put some of these principles into practice.

Activity: Adding Contacts to a Directory

You need to add contacts to the directory that you are creating, stored as an array of names. The app should return an array of contacts when requested.

The reason for this is to gain a better overall understanding of how to use OOP in practical applications.

Follow these steps to perform this activity:

1. Create a directory structure.
2. Create a directory named Contacts.
3. In this directory, create a directory named App.
4. Within the App directory, create three more directories:
   - Models
   - views
   - Controllers
5. Within the Models directory, create a file named Contact.php.
   1. In the Contact.php file, open PHP, and create a namespace:
      ```php
      <?php namespace App\Models;
      ```
   2. Define a class called Contact:
      ```php
      class Contact
      {
      }
      ```
   3. In this class, define a public method called getContacts(); it should return an array of names:
      ```php
      class Contact
      {
          public function getContacts()
      {
              return ['joe', 'bob', 'kerry', 'dave'];
          }
      }
      ```
6. Within the Controllers directory, create a file named Contacts.php.
7. In the Contacts.php file, open PHP, and add a namespace:
   ```php
   <?php namespace App\Controllers;
   ```
8. Import the Contact model with a use statement:
   ```php
   use App\Models\Contact;
   ```

9. An alias may be used in this scenario, written as follows (assuming that an alias for Contact would be `Name`):

```
Use App\Models\Contact as Name;
```

Define a class named Contacts:

```
class Contacts
{

}
```

10. Create a public function called `index()`, and within that method, create a local variable called `contacts`, and create a new instance of the `contact` class (this is known as the instantiation of a class):

```
class Contacts
{
    public function index()
    {
        $contact = new Contact();
    }
}
```

11. Create a local variable called `contacts` using the assignment operator, call the `contacts` object that you created an instance of in the previous step, add -> (this is known as an arrow notation), and call the method `getContacts()`:

```
public function index()
{
    $contact = new Contact();
    $contacts = $contact->getContacts();
}
```

Summary

In this chapter, we have created a model and a controller, where the controller `Contacts` class instantiates the model `Contact` class. To achieve this, we created a basic MVC folder structure, separating the controls from the data source. We successfully used a `namespace`, a use statement, a method, an access modifier, an object, and a class. We have now witnessed the power of a framework.

In the next chapter, you will create a working framework of your own. We will be looking at how to set up a project development environment, graceful error reporting, and handing using the Whoops library. We will also be implementing the configuration classes, default classes, and how to set up routing.

6

Building a PHP Framework

In the previous chapter, we have created a model and a controller, where the controller `Contacts` class instantiates the model `Contact` class. We successfully used a `namespace`, a `use` statement, a method, an access modifier, an object, and a class. We have witnessed the power of a framework in the previous chapter.

In this chapter, we will be building an MVC framework from scratch. A framework is really just a way to organize the code and structure it. Starting from an empty directory, we will build an entire working framework as a starting point for more complex applications.

 In the previous chapter, we retrieved data from an array. In this chapter, we will retrieve it from the database.

By the end of this chapter, you will be able to:

- Build a basic PHP MVC framework
- Implement the OOP concepts covered in the previous chapters
- Identify how to route a controller to a specified URI
- Interact with the database with PHP Data Objects (PDO)
- Work with HTML to build and create reusable pages (views)

We will also be implementing the OOP concepts that we have covered in previous chapters, including, but not restricted to, namespaces, use statements, objects and classes, access modifiers, and methods.

We will learn how to route a controller to a specified URL and work with HTML to build and create reusable pages (views). Finally, we will interact with the database using a PDO.

Setting up a Project Development Environment

This section is concerned with setting up the project development environment.

This is all about setting up the index, the .htaccess file, creating the web root, setting up the composer, and setting up the app directory.

- **The index** is the bootstrap file of the framework; this is ultimately where all requests are received. A request is made, for example, when the user inputs a URL into the address bar.

- **.htaccess** is the mod rewrite engine that passes all requests to the index file.

- **Web root** is the public folder that would be accessible to the browser, as well as for storing the index and .htaccess of all the web application's assets. This would include images, CSS, and JavaScript files.

- **Composer** is a package manager for managing libraries of code which the system is dependent on.

- **App directory** is your application; it is where your views, models, controllers, and helpers will be stored. Helpers are compact methods that help with single common tasks developers come across frequently. It is common that a developer may find themselves repeating the same tasks and will create a helper class with single or several methods to help with this task. This could be formatting dates, performing specific calculations, and many more.

 The boot symbolizes what the process of setting up a framework is commonly known as bootstrapping. This is not to be confused with the popular CSS Grid named Bootstrap. This essentially tightly ties all core parts of the framework together.

Error Reporting Using Composer and Whoops

For this project, we will be using the Whoops library to handle errors. The Whoops library is a tool for examining errors that may occur in your projects. This library is packaged and made available for other developers to use in their projects.

Using Whoops, when an error occurs in PHP, you will be able to see this display information as opposed to standard bland error reporting from the server:

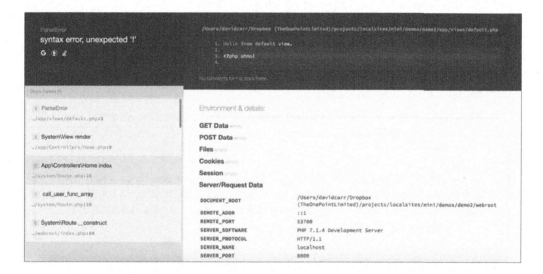

Composer will manage the use of this dependency as it is considered among PHP developers a very widely used and a very popular package manager.

Composer is a tool for dependency management in PHP. It allows you to declare the libraries your project depends on and it will manage (install/update) them for you. To install Composer, go to `https://getcomposer.org/download/`.

Imagine a scenario where you have to install a dependency for PHP, and for installing that dependency, you need to install other overhead dependencies. Composer helps you in handling this problem. It is used to handle all the work for you to install a library, as it downloads all the libraries and dependencies together.

Setting up Composer

We'll look at setting up Composer in this section. To do this, follow these steps:

1. Create a folder to store the framework files.

 Feel free to call your folder anything you like, as long as it's all in lowercase without any spaces.

2.

   o app holds the application files

   o system holds the core framework files

   o webroot will hold the publicly accessible files

3. Next, we will set up Composer. Create a file in the root of your framework folder called composer.json.

   This file holds a JSON object that will autoload classes as we need them. We will be using PSR-4 autoloading.

 PSR-4 autoloading will load a class based on its namespace when it's being used. For instance, new App\Models\Contact() will tell Composer to autoload a file called Contact that is stored in the folder app\Models.

4. Open composer.json and create an App and System definition.

5. This will tell Composer that everything we call a namespace, with either App or System to look for the class in the app or system folders.

6. We are also loading a third-party package called Whoops. We load this package by including it as a dependency in a require block:

```
{
    "autoload": {
        "psr-4": {
            "App\\" : "app/",
            "System\\" : "system/"
        }
    },
```

```
    "require": {
        "filp/whoops": "^2.1"
    }
}
```

7. Save `composer.json`. Now, inside `webroot`, create two files: `index.php` and `.htaccess`.

8. Open `.htaccess`.

9. For security reasons, if a folder does not contain an `index` file, we don't want its contents displayed in a browser. To disable directory browsing, enter:

```
Options -Indexes
```

10. Next, a check is made to ensure mod rewrite is enabled:

```
<IfModule mod_rewrite.c>
//more code
</IfModule>
```

 mod rewrite provides a rule-based rewriting engine to rewrite requested URLs on the fly. It helps to make URLs, so `index.php?page` can become `/page`.

11. Next, turn on the rewriting engine and set the base to the root of this folder:

```
RewriteEngine On
RewriteBase /
```

12. To force HTTPS, you can uncomment the # below, but only do this on a server that has HTTP enabled.

13. Next, define the rewrite conditions.

Note

This is to ignore trailing slashes and folder and files that exist. Only dynamic files should be routed, for example, URLs that do not exist as physical files.

The last rule passes all requests to `index.php?$1`. The `$1` is the request after the first / in the requested URL.

`RewriteCond` basically means "execute the next `RewriteRule` only if this is true".

The `RewriteRule` basically means that if the request is done that matches `^(.+)$` (matches any URL except the server root), it will be rewritten as `index.php?$1`, which means a request for contact will be rewritten as `index.php?contact`:

RewriteRule ^(.*)$ index.php?$1 [QSA,L]

QSA means that this flag forces the rewriting engine to append a query string part in the substitution string to the existing one instead of replacing it.

The Secure Sockets Layer (SSL) creates an encrypted connection between your web server and your web browser. This stops any data being intercepted from your machine to the web server. It's recommended to use HTTPS.

The complete file should look like this:

```
# Disable directory snooping
Options -Indexes

<IfModule mod_rewrite.c>

    # Uncomment the rule below to force HTTPS (SSL)
..........
    RewriteRule ^(.*)$ index.php?$1 [QSA,L]
</IfModule>
```

For full code snippet, refer to Lesson 6.php file in the code files folder.

14. Save the file. Now, open `index.php`.

15. First, start php and then do a check to determine if `vendor/autoload.php` exists (it won't exist yet) and require the file.

> This is an important step. The autoload.php file will only exist once the Composer has been initialized. Checking before requiring the file is a precaution used to avoid a fatal error.

16. We should inform the user what Composer is requesting and where to go and get it. We do this by using an `else` clause:

```php
if(file_exists('../vendor/autoload.php')){
    require '../vendor/autoload.php';
} else {
    echo "<h1>Please install via composer.json</h1>";
    echo "<p>Install Composer instructions: <a href='https://
getcomposer.org/doc/00-intro.md#globally'>https://getcomposer.org/
doc/00-intro.md#globally</a></p>";
    echo "<p>Once composer is installed navigate to the working
directory in your terminal/command prompt and enter 'composer
install'</p>";
    exit;
}
```

17. Next, we will set our environment.

18. We will define a constant called `ENVIRONMENT` and give it a value of development. When going into `production`, set the `environment` to `production`.

> When in production, you do not want to show errors. Having an environment constant is a good way to set what the environment of the application is:
>
> ```php
> define('ENVIRONMENT', 'development');
> ```

19. Now, based on the `environment` constant, we can set the appropriate level of error reporting:

```php
if (defined('ENVIRONMENT')){
    switch (ENVIRONMENT){
        case 'development':
            error_reporting(E_ALL);
        break;
        case 'production':
            error_reporting(0);
        break;
        default:
            exit('The application environment is not set
correctly.');
    }
}
```

In development mode, all errors will be displayed, but in production, no errors will be displayed.

The complete file looks like this:

```php
<?php
if(file_exists('../vendor/autoload.php')){
    require '../vendor/autoload.php';
} else {
......
            error_reporting(0);
        break;
default:
            exit('The application environment is not set
correctly.');
    }

}
```

For full code snippet, refer to Lesson 6.php file in the code files folder.

A new folder will now have been created called vendor. This folder is where Composer installs its required files and any third-party dependencies.

20. You can now go back to your browser and reload the page. You should now see a blank page.

This means Composer is working, but we haven't yet requested anything to be loaded.

Errors in view when the Whoops package is turned on will display the errors on the screen with a full stack trace of how the framework has executed the code along the way. This can help developers isolate the issue by following the path that their code has traveled on.

Activity: Using Composer to Install Dependencies

Suppose you are working on a PHP project and you need a lot of dependencies for your project. You are on a strict deadline, yet, you cannot proceed ahead before adding those dependencies. You discovered that you can use Composer to install dependencies automatically. You now need to install Composer.

The aim of this activity is to get you acquainted with Composer installation.

To perform this activity, follow these steps:

1. Run the framework by opening Terminal or command prompt.

2. If on Windows, navigate to the `framework` folder and launch the php server:

   `php -S localhost:8000 -t Webroot`

The `-S` means that run the server and use localhost:8000 as it's address, and `-t Webroot` sets the document `root` to the `Webroot` folder.

The Terminal output will look like this (some of the details will be different on your system):

```
PHP 7.1.4 Development Server started at Wed Nov 29 20:37:27 2017
Listening on http://localhost:8000
Document root is /Users/davidcarr/Dropbox /projects/localsites/
framework/webroot
Press Ctrl-C to quit.
```

3. Now, go to `http://localhost:8000` and you will see the Composer instructions we wrote in the `else` statement in `index.php`.

4. This is because we have not yet set up Composer. We do this by typing the following in the Terminal:

```
composer install
```

The output will be as follows:

```
Loading composer repositories with package information
Updating dependencies (including require-dev)
Package operations: 2 installs, 0 updates, 0 removals
  - Installing psr/log (1.0.2) Loading from cache
  - Installing filp/whoops (2.1.14) Downloading: 100%
filp/whoops suggests installing symfony/var-dumper (Pretty print
complex values better with var-dumper available)
filp/whoops suggests installing whoops/soap (Formats errors as
SOAP responses)
Writing lock file
Generating autoload files
```

5. Observe that a new folder will now have been created called `vendor`. This folder is where Composer installs its required files and any third-party dependencies.

6. Now, go back to your browser and reload the page.

> You should now see a blank page.
>
> This means Composer is working, but we haven't yet requested anything to be loaded.

7. Go back to index.php in your editor and add these lines at the bottom of the file:

```
//initiate config
$config = App\Config::get();

new System\Route($config);
```

This will load our `config` class and set up our routing.

8. Save `index.php` and create a new file called `Config.php` inside the `app` folder.

 Take care to name the file `Config` and `not config`. Case sensitivity is important on Unix-based systems such as Mac and Linux.

We have reached the end of this section. We have learned how to bootstrap an application, which allows for a single entry point, and how to use Composer to autoload the classes. We covered how errors are handled and finally, we covered the build process of the framework.

In the next section, we will set up the configuration class and will also set up routing.

Configuration Class, Default Classes, and Routing

In this section, we will learn about the `configuration` class, and we will also be setting up routing.

We will be setting up the `config` class. This will be located in the root of the `app` folder. The `config` class stores the default controller, the `default` method to be loaded, and the database credentials. In the `index` file at the beginning, you will be passing the `config` class to the `route` class. The `route` class controls what is to be loaded and when. The focus for now is the `configuration` class and routing. The other components will be looked at in more detail in later sections.

The configuration class is an array of options for the framework including the following:

- Database source credentials
- Paths to default controllers
- Paths to default methods

In this section, we will also create a view class which is responsible for loading views, which enables a place for the presentation layer to be displayed.

When setting up routing, we are informing the framework where to look in the files system that matches the URL.

When loading the correct file, this will be the required controller class. We will activate the required method, the required model, and the required view.

We will do all of this so the user can see in their browser what they have requested from simply clicking on a link, which is otherwise known as making a request to the server.

Then, we will create the route class, which takes segments from the URL so it knows which controller and method to load and parameters to pass.

For instance, the URL http://localhost:8000/contacts/view/2 says *Go to the contacts controller view method*. In this case, the number 2 represents a parameter being passed through to the view method.

 The configuration class is more commonly known by developers as the config class.

Configuration is a natural place that users might look to for help on understanding how to remember important details about their framework project. It is advisable to developers to develop a system to remember details about their projects.

This can be helpful if they plan to make their project open source. It can also be helpful to the developer if they need to remember details about a project at a later date, as months, even years, can go by before the developer needs to revisit the project.

What kind of details could these be?

- **Version number** – Over time, the developer may make additions and improvements, which can affect the very core of the code base. Knowing what version you are working with can help you select the proper approach to a programming problem later on.

- **Credits** – It is good practice to credit the work of other developers whose work you have used. If you fail to do so and you may receive an unhappy email from an uncredited developer.

- **Author details** – Users of open source projects may benefit from contact details of the original developer. Annoyed uncredited developers need somewhere to send that unhappy email.

```php
Config.php
<?php
/**
 * Config - the Global Configuration loaded BEFORE the Nova Application starts.
 *
 * @author name of author here - name@authorwebsite.com
 * @version 3.0
 */


/**
 * PREFIX to be used in Database calls or storing Session data, default is 'projectName_'
 */
define('PREFIX', 'projectName_');

/**
 * Setup the Config API Mode.
 * For using the 'database' mode, you need to have a database, with a table generated by 'scripts/nova_options'
 */
define('CONFIG_STORE', 'database'); // Supported: "files", "database"
```

Here is an example of a Config class

Loading a View File

We'll look at an example to demonstrate the ability to load up view files once this section is complete. However, no views have been created at this stage, so a custom 404 page is used in its place.

The example in this section loads up the framework in a browser. Initially, you will see a 404 message in the browser as the view cannot be found. This is because the default controller does not exist.

A sample `404` php file exists inside the `views` folder with the message "the file cannot be found". Save the file and refresh the browser of the newly created 404 page.

9. Open php and give the file a `namespace` of App.

 The class belongs to the App namespace as it is stored inside the **app** folder.

10. Next, define a class called `Config` and create a method called `get`.

 The `get` method needs to return an array. The keys of the array will be the settings used for the routing and database credentials:

For full code snippet, refer to `Lesson 6.php` file in the code files folder.

```php
<?php namespace App;

class Config {
......
    public static function get()
            'db_name'     => 'mini',
            'db_username' => 'root',
            'db_password' => '',
        ];
    }
}
```

 The preceding namespace definition holds the path of App\Controllers. Note the double backslash — this is because backslashes are often escaped, so using a double stops it from being escaped.

The namespace definition, default controller, and default method will become clear when we write the router.

11. Finally, set up the database properties.

12. Set up the database properties for the type of database to be used and its location, followed by the database name and the username and password to access the database.

13. You will need to access a MySQL database in order to create a database. To set up a native database, MariaDB is recommended. To download MariaDB, follow the instructions at `https://mariadb.com/downloads/mariadb-tx`.

> In this example, we have a database called mini, and my username is root. We do not have a password, so we leave it blank.

14. Save the `Config.php` file.

15. Before the `routing` class can be set up, we need to create a `View` class. This class will be responsible for loading the `view` files and also showing a 404 page when a URL cannot be found.

16. In system, create a new file called `View.php`.

17. Open php and set the namespace to `System`. Next, define a class called `View` and create a method called `render` that accepts two parameters, `$path` and `$data`.

> `$path` will hold the path of the requested file.
>
> `$data` will hold the content to be passed to the `view` file.
>
> `$data` is optional; note it has a default value of `false`. This means if there is only one parameter passed to the `render` method, then the data will not be used.
>
> Inside the method ID, a Boolean checks for `$data`. If it's `false`, it is ignored; otherwise, the data is looped through using a `foreach` loop. On each loop, the data is extracted to a local variable.

18. After the loop, set the relative path to where the view files will be stored, in this case `app/views/` followed by the requested view.

19. Finally, a check is made to ensure the `view` file exists and requires it, otherwise an error is generated:

> For full code snippet, refer to `Lesson 6.php` file in the code files folder.

```php
<?php
namespace System;

/*
 * View - load template pages
 *
 */
class View {
.......
        } else {
            die("View: $path not found!");
        }


    }
}
```

20. Save the file and create a new file called `Route.php` inside the `system` folder.

21. Open php and set the namespace to `System`.

22. The `View` class we've just created needs to be available to this class. To import it, add:

```php
use System\View;
```

 This loads the `View` file. The reason PHP knows where to find the file is because of the namespace, which is Composer in action. Being able to import classes this way is really helpful.

23. Now, create a class called `Route` and a method called `__construct`, which expects a parameter called `$config`:

```php
<?php namespace System;

use System\View;
```

```
class Route
{
    public function __construct($config)
    {
```

24. Now, set up the following variables:

```
$url        = explode('/', trim($_SERVER['REQUEST_URI'], '/'));
$controller = !empty($url[0]) ? $url[0] : $config['default_
controller'];
$method     = !empty($url[1]) ? $url[1] : $config['default_
method'];
$args       = !empty($url[2]) ? array_slice($url, 2) : array();
$class      = $config['namespace'].$controller;
```

The $url will hold an array from the requested route in the form of /page/requested. This is how it works: When explode is run, it finds a forward slash in the requested URI, which the $_SERVER makes available.

Next, the $controller method uses a ternary operator to check if the 0 index of $url exists, otherwise the default_controller defined in the Config class is used.

The $method checks for the existence of a $url[1], otherwise it reads from the config class.

$args will get all other indexes of $url after the first 2.

$class holds the path to the controllers as set in the Config class.

What these parameters do is get the Controller, Method, and parameters from the requested URL. For instance:

http://localhost:8000/contacts/view/2

This results in:

Contacts = Contacts class.

View = View method inside the contacts class.

2 = A parameter passed to the method.

If the requested URL is http::://localhost:8000/, then no controller or method is requested, so the default controller and method will be used, as set in system\Config.php.

25. After these variables have been set up, a check is made, that is, if the class does not exist, call a method of not_found that exists within the Route class (not yet set up):

```
//check the class exists
if (! class_exists($class)) {
    return $this->not_found();
}
```

26. Next, the method is checked to ensure it exists:

```
//check the method exists
if (! method_exists($class, $method)) {
    return $this->not_found();
}
```

27. Next, set up an instance of the class:

```
//create an instance of the controller
$classInstance = new $class;
```

28. Run the class by calling call_user_func_array and pass in an array of the class instance and method, and pass any arguments as a second parameter:

```
//call the controller and its method and pass in any arguments
call_user_func_array(array($classInstance, $method), $args);
```

29. If a route is called that does not exist, a not_found method is needed. This calls the render method and passes 404 as the parameter. This will attempt to load app/view/404.php, should it exist:

```
//class or method not found return a 404 view
public function not_found()
{
    $view = new View();
    return $view->render('404');
}
```

The full class looks like this:

 For full code snippet, refer to Lesson 6.php file in the code files folder.

```php
<?php namespace System;

use System\View;

class Route
.......
    {
        $view = new View();
        return $view->render('404');
    }
  }
}
```

Manipulating the Output

This section shows you how to manipulate the output of the previous example. Here are the steps to do it:

1. Load up the framework `http://localhost:8000` and you will see the following output:

    ```
    View: 404 not found!
    ```

 This is because the default controller does not yet exist and neither does app/views/404.php.

2. Create a `views` folder inside the `app` folder and create a file called `404.php`. Enter a message such as 'The file cannot be found.' and save the file.

3. Reload the framework in your browser and you will now see your message.

In this section, we covered the `configuration` class wherein we saw how the configuration class sits on top of the `root` folder. We also saw how to set up routing, where we performed the loading of a `view` page.

In the next section, we will cover the base controller, which defines the main functionality of the MVC framework.

Base Controller, Default States, and Routing

The base controller class — because of the nature of an MVC framework — requires a default state.

A default view is loaded by a default method within a default controller class.

From this default controller class, all other controllers across the system are loaded.

This creation of the default Controller class and default method will be the focus of what we are building during in this section.

 It is not essential that the model be included as the controller, and the view can work independently without a data source.

Setting up Base Controller, Default States, and Routing

In this section, we'll look at setting up base controller, default states, and routing. The following are the steps:

Views:

1.   Now, let's set up the default view. Create a file called default.php inside app\views and write the content of `Hello from default view.` or any other message.

     This will be displayed when on the framework's home page.

Controllers:

Before we can start building our application controllers, we need a base controller that all other controllers can extend from. The reason for this is so the controllers can make use of any properties or methods defined in the base controller.

2.   Create a new file called BaseController.php and save it in the system folder.

3.   Open php and set the namespace to System. Define a class called BaseController.

4. Define two class properties called $view and $url. Both of these properties will have an access modifier of public, meaning anywhere the BaseController is used, the properties will be available.

5. Next, create a construct method, then set up a new instance of the View class. This is so $this->view can be used to call the render method of the view within extended controllers.

6. Next, assign a method of getUrl() to the property $this->url. This will call another method to get the current URL.

7. Now, a check is run on the environment mode. If it's set to development, then a new instance of the Whoops error handler is created. This Whoops class is brought in by Composer, as defined by the composer.json file.

   The Whoops class will give a rich error stack trace when errors occur with the code when run in a browser.

8. Finally, a getUrl() method is defined that will return the requested URL:

 For full code snippet, refer to Lesson 6.php file in the code files folder.

```php
<?php namespace System;

use System\View;

class BaseController
{

  public $view;
.........
    $url = isset($_SERVER['REQUEST_URI']) ? rtrim($_
SERVER['REQUEST_URI'], '/') : NULL;
    $url = filter_var($url, FILTER_SANITIZE_URL);
    return $this->url = $url;
  }


}
```

Home Controller:

1. In app/Config.php, we set the default_controller to be home:

```
//set default controller
'default_controller' => 'Home',

//set default method
'default_method' => 'index',
```

2. Let's create this now. Create a Controllers folder inside the app folder and create a file called Home.php.

 All classes should start with a capital letter and each subsequent word should be capitalized.

3. Open php and set the namespace to App\Controllers. This namespace references the folder structure.

4. Next, import the BaseController by calling its namespace and call name.

5. Define a class called Home and extend the BaseController.

   This will allow the Home controller to have access to $this->view and loading the views.

6. Create a method called index and then return $this->view->render and pass the filename to be loaded.

7. In this case, pass in default, and app\views\default.php will be loaded:

```php
<?php
namespace App\Controllers;

use System\BaseController;

class Home extends BaseController
{
  public function index()
  {
    return $this->view->render('default');
  }
}
```

Activity: Exploring the Results

We will now be able to see the output of the task, as seen in the demo file. Follow these steps to do so:

1. Open your framework in the browser `http://localhost:8000` and you will see your default view file being loaded.

2. Remember that Whoops class? Well, let's see that in action. Open your `default.php` view file and add this code at the end of the file. Open php and write something, but not in a string. The code should look as follows:

   ```
   Hello from default view.
   <?php ohno!
   ```

3. Now, save and reload the page in the browser and you will see:

   This page tells you what the error is, but also shows a code snippet of where the problem is and a complete stack trace so that you can trace the journey from execution to failure:

4. Now, remove your modifications from `default.php` so it only contains your original content, save, and reload the page again. You will see your page loading normally again.

5. Now, let's look at how to access a new method. In your Home controller, create a new method called `packt` that loads a view called `packt`.

6. Create a new view file in app\views called packt.php and enter the text 'Hello from Packt!'

7. Load up the page by going to home/packt http://localhost:8000/home/packt.

You will now see the contents of your packt view file.

In this section, we have gained a better understanding of the role default states play in our project. This project requires these base methods to initially run and to extend from.

We have gained experience by building default states including baseController and baseMethod.

In the next section, we will learn about PDO, a lightweight interface for gaining access to databases in PHP.

Working with PDO

In this section, we will be creating the PDO wrapper and using a database as a data source from our model.

From this section, we will gain the ability to use a database within our framework project.

Six methods will be covered here.

We have a get method — this is for creating a connection to the database and making sure it is a singleton instance, meaning it can only ever have one instance:

- We have a raw method for running raw, unsecured queries
- A select method for running secure queries to select records from the database
- An insert method to create new records
- An update method to update records
- A delete method to delete records
- A truncate method to empty a table

What this does is allow your CRUD to work. Without this class, CRUD functionality would not be possible.

The base model is where we are creating the database connection using the database helper.

This will allow other model classes to extend from this model and use a database connection. This only consists of one single method:

Construct:

This is responsible for passing the config to the database helper to create the database connection.

Now, we are ready to start using the database.

 Database access: If you find that you do not have access to a database client or PHP admin web interface, then a fallback option is included that all students may use to create a database and insert data.

The upcoming section is all about creating the first model inside the apps folder. We will create the model `contact.php` and talk about best practices and naming conventions, as well as extending from the base model created earlier, alongside setting up a method to display records from a database.

Next, we will create a `contact` controller that extends from the base controller. That imports the contact model before calling that on an index method and passing the records from the model to the view. In that view, we will look through the records and display them one per line.

We then open up the browser and go to the contacts controller to see the contacts being displayed on the page.

To load a different controller, it's the same process as described in the previous subtopic. Create a controller, set its namespace, and define the classes to exist in the base controller, and either have an index method that loads when calling the controller name or use a different name and access it by calling your controllername/methodname.

We're nearly at the end of the framework setup. Right now, we can create controllers and methods to load pages and pass data to views. For a static site, this is great—it will keep your code organized and running quickly—but one vital component missing is the ability to use a database.

On that note, we're going to create a database helper. This is a fancy name for a class that's stored in a common folder named `helpers`. Helpers are classes that don't fit in with Controllers or Models, but are standalone classes to extend functionality.

The database helper will have six methods:

- `get()` – Set up the database connection
- `raw()` – Run a raw, unsecure query
- `select()` – Run a query to select records from a database
- `insert()` – Create new records
- `update()` – Update existing records
- `delete()` – Delete existing records
- `truncate()` – Empty a table

Creating a Contact Controller and Viewing the Records

In this section, we will start creating our contact controller. Follow these steps to do so:

1. First, create a folder called `Helpers` inside of the `app` folder and create a new file called `Database.php`.

2. Open php and set the namespace as `App\Helpers`.

3. Next, we need to import PDO.

 PDO is a database abstraction layer; it's a wrapper that supports 12 different database engines including MySQL. It's what we will be using to talk to the database.

4. To import PDO, use a `use` statement:

```php
<?php
namespace App\Helpers;

use PDO;
```

5. Next, define a class called `Database` that extends `PDO`. Inside the class create a property called `$instances` and set it as an array datatype.

6. The $instances property will be used to ensure there is only ever a single database connection in use:

```
class Database extends PDO
{
protected static $instances = array();
```

7. Next, create a method called get() that accepts a pram called $config. This will be the Config that is set up in app\Config.php.

8. Inside this method, set up the local variables to hold the database credentials. These values will be extracted from the $config array.

9. Then, create a variable called $id. This will hold all the database local variables to create an identifier. Next, a check is performed to check if the $instance property already has this $id.

10. If $instances does have the $id, then it will return the $instance, otherwise a new PDO connection is attempted.

When connecting to PDO, the database credentials are passed and the charset is set to UTF-8.

11. On the next line, the error mode is set to exception. This means any exceptions will be caused and displayed.

12. Now, set the $instance to the current connection and return $instance:

For full code snippet, refer to Lesson 6.php file in the code files folder.

```
GET method

public static function get($config)
{
  // Group information
.......
  // Setting Database into $instances to avoid duplication
  self::$instances[$id] = $instance;

  //return the pdo instance
  return $instance;

}
```

RAW method

1. Create a method called `raw`. This is a very simple method. It accepts a single parameter which is an SQL statement. The `$sql` is passed to `$this->query`, which will then run the query directly:

 This is useful for executing queries that you don't need to be secure. If no checking is done, the query will be executed as is and the result is returned.

```
public function raw($sql)
{
  return $this->query($sql);
}
```

SELECT method:

1. Next, create a method called `select()`. This will accept four parameters:
   - `$sql` – The SQL query
   - `$array` – Any keys to be bound to the query (optional)
   - `$fetchMode` – Sets the PDO fetch mode default to object (optional)
   - `$class` – Used to specify a class to be used in conjunction with the fetch mode

Inside the method so you don't have to write
`$this->db->select('SELECT * FROM table')` we're going
to add select to the SQL query providing it's not already there. This
is done by changing the case to lowercase and then using `substr`
to check the first seven letters of the `$sql`. It it's not equal to
select, then add select to the start.

2. Next, prepare the query. This will set up the SQL query without running it. Next, the $array is looped over and any values are assigned to the particular datatype. If the value is an INT, then a datatype of PARAM_INT is used, otherwise the datatype will use string.

3. Finally, the execution is run. This passes the $sql to the server and the binded $array keys separately, meaning there is no way a SQL injection can ever happen, resulting in a secure query.

   After the query has been executed, the response is then retuned.
   By default, an object is returned:

 For full code snippet, refer to `Lesson 6.php` file in the
code files folder.

```php
public function select($sql, $array = array(), $fetchMode =
PDO::FETCH_OBJ, $class = '')
{
......
    return $stmt->fetchAll($fetchMode);
  }
}
```

INSERT method

1. To insert new records into the database, an insert query is required. Create a new method called insert with two parameters:
   - $table – The table name
   - $data – An array of keys and values to insert into the $table

2. Sort the $data array by using ksort($data).

3. Next, extract all the array keys to a variable called $fieldNames. This is done using implode and setting a comma between each key and running array_keys() against the $data.

4. Now, do the same again, this time adding , : as the implode options, and save this to a variable called $fieldValues.

5. Then, using $this->prepare, a SQL command can be written that will set the $fieldNames into the value of $fieldValues for the $table. Loop over the $data and bind the values.

6. Lastly, return the ID of the last inserted record. This is useful when you need the primary key as soon as the record is inserted:

```php
public function insert($table, $data)
{
  ksort($data);
  $fieldNames = implode(',', array_keys($data));
  $fieldValues = ':'.implode(', :', array_keys($data));

  $stmt = $this->prepare("INSERT INTO $table ($fieldNames) VALUES
($fieldValues)");

  foreach ($data as $key => $value) {
    $stmt->bindValue(":$key", $value);
  }
  $stmt->execute();
 return $this->lastInsertId();
}
```

UPDATE method

1. Next, create a method called update with three parameters:
   - o $table – The table name
   - o $data – An array of data to update
   - o $where – An array of the key and value to put a condition, for example,
     ['id' => 2], where id is equal to 2

2. Sort the $data and then extract the $data.

3. Inside the loop, append to a variable called $fieldData. Add $key = :$key. Next, remove any whitespace to the right by calling trim().

4. Next, loop through the $where array. On each loop, assign the $key = :$key. This creates a list of placeholders for the binding to catch later.

5. Again, trim any whitespace to the right, then use $this->prepare and write the update SQL pass in the table name followed by the fieldDetails and the WhereDetails.

6. Next, bind the keys to the :$key placeholders and execute the query.

7. The last step is to return a rowCount(). This is the number of records that have been updated:

> For full code snippet, refer to the Lesson 6.php file in the code files folder.

```php
public function update($table, $data, $where)

{

    ksort($data);

    $fieldDetails = null;
    .......
    }
    $stmt->execute();
    return $stmt->rowCount();
}
```

DELETE method

1. Create a new method called delete with three parameters:

    o $table – The name of the table

    o $where – An array of key values to determine the where condition

    o $limit – The number of records to delete, Default value is 1, pass null to remove a number limit

2. Inside the method, sort the $where loop through the $where and set up the placeholders from the key and values of the array.

3. Prepare the query and write the SQL command passing, in the $table, $where, and $limit.

4. The last step is to return a rowCount(). This is the number of records that have been deleted:

 For full code snippet, refer to Lesson 6.php file in the code files folder.

```php
public function delete($table, $where, $limit = 1)
{
    ksort($where);

........

    $stmt->execute();
    return $stmt->rowCount();
}
```

TRUNCATE method

1. The last method to make is called truncate, which accepts one parameter, $table:

    o $table – The table name

2. Inside the method, call $this->exec and the SQL command TRUNCATE TABLE $table. This will empty the table, resulting in no records. All primary keys will be reset to 0, as if the table had never been used:

```php
public function truncate($table)
{
    return $this->exec("TRUNCATE TABLE $table");
}
```

The full class looks like this:

 For full code snippet, refer to Lesson 6.php file in the code files folder.

```php
<?php namespace App\Helpers;

use PDO;
class Database extends PDO
{
    /**
     * @var array Array of saved databases for reusing
     */
     */
......
    {
        return $this->exec("TRUNCATE TABLE $table");
    }
}
```

3. Save this class. This is a complex class, and the rest of the code we will be writing is much simpler. In the next few pages, we will be using the database helpers, and the purpose and use of methods will become clear as they are used.

Base Model

1. Our next task is to create a basemodel class that will connect to the database using the Database helper and return the instance. This will allow other model classes to extend from this class and use the database connection.

2. Create a file called BaseModel.php inside the system folder.

3. Open php and set the namespace to System.

4. Import the Config class and the Database helper class by calling their namespaces in a use statement.

5. Define the class and call BaseModel, then create a protected property called $db. This is what other models will use to interact with the database.

6. Create a __construct() method. This will run as soon as the class is instantiated. Inside this method, create a local variable called $config and assign it Config::get().

7. Next, create a new instance of the Database helper and call the get method and pass in $config.

The class looks like this:

 For full code snippet, refer to `Lesson 6.php` file in the code files folder.

```php
<?php namespace System;
/*
 * model - the base model
 *
....... .
//connect to PDO here.
$this->db = Database::get($config);
}
}
```

8. Now, we are ready to start using the database. Before we continue with our code base, open your database you connected to earlier, either using phpmyadmin or a MySQL client, or using Terminal.

9. Create a database—we will call it mini—and create a table called `contacts` with two columns: ID and name.

 If you don't have a MySQL client, you can use Terminal by typing:

mysql –u root

Replace root with your database username. Root is the default. I have MariaDB installed by default. There is no password, but should you need to enter the password, pass in the password flag –p:

mysql –u root –p

10. Create a new database.

11. Create database mini.

12. Select that database:

```
use mini
```

 This now uses the database called mini.

13. The database is empty, so let's create a table called contacts:

```
create table contacts (
`id` int(11) unsigned NOT NULL AUTO_INCREMENT,
`name` varchar(255) DEFAULT NULL,
PRIMARY KEY (`id`)
) ENGINE=InnoDB DEFAULT CHARSET=latin1;
```

To see a list of your tables:

```
show tables;

+-----------------+
| Tables_in_mini |
+-----------------+
| contacts        |
+-----------------+
1 row in set (0.00 sec)

Insert data into the table
insert into contacts (name) values('Dave');
insert into contacts (name) values('Markus');

this will insert the records to see the contents of the table:
select * from contacts;

+----+--------+
| id | name   |
+----+--------+
|  1 | Dave   |
|  2 | Markus |
+----+--------+
2 rows in set (0.00 sec)
```

With these few commands, the database has been created, as well as a table, which has been populated with two records.

Activity: Creating and Executing the Model

We have created the contact Controller and viewed the result. We now need to implement the Model for our application.

The aim of this activity is to implement the Model for our application.

Getting back to the framework, we are now ready to create our first Model. Follow these steps to do it:

1. Inside the app folder, create a new folder called Models. This is where all the models will be stored. Now, create a new file called Contact.php.

    [It's a best practice to name your models as a singular record, so in this case, Contact represents a table of Contacts.]

2. In Contact.php, open php and set the namespace to App\Models;.

3. Import the BaseModel and create a class called Contact and extend the BaseModel.

4. Create a method called getContacts(). This method will be used to get all contacts stored in the database.

5. Call $this->db->select() to call the select method of the database helper and write the SQL * FROM contacts.

    [It's a best practice to write commands like SELECT, FROM, WHERE, GROUP BY, and ORDER BY in capitals, so make it clear in your code what the commands are.]

The model looks like this:

```php
<?php
namespace App\Models;
use System\BaseModel;

class Contact extends BaseModel
{
  public function getContacts()
  {
    return $this->db->select('* FROM contacts);
  }
}
```

6. Now, we need to run this model. The best place for this is inside a controller. Create a new controller called Contacts inside the app\Controllers folder.

    This class extends from the BaseController and has a method called index:

```php
<?php
namespace App\Controllers;

use System\BaseController;

class Contacts extends BaseController
{
  public function index()
  {


  }
}
```

    Let's inform the index method to load a view called contacts/index:

```php
public function index()
{
  return $this->view->render('contacts/index');
}
```

7. Create a folder called contacts in app\views and create a file called index. php.

    If you run this now and go to localhost:8000/contacts, you will get a blank page or see the contents of contacts/index.php, providing you've entered some content.

8. Going back to the `contacts controller`, we need to import the `contact` model. We do this by using a `use` statement and setting the namespace to the model:

```
use App\Models\Contact;
```

9. Inside the `index` method, create a new instance of the `contact` model and call the `getContacts()` method. Assign it to a variable called `$records`:

```
$contacts = new Contact();
$records = $contacts->getContacts();
```

10. Next, pass the `$records` to the `view`:

```
return $this->view->render('contacts/index', compact('records'));
```

 Using `compact()` is a clean way to put a string name representing the variable. This will read `$records` and pass it to the view:

Inside app\views\contacts\index.php

11. Open `php` and check that `$records` exists and then do a `foreach` loop and loop through each record. `echo` the `name` key from the `$row` object. Add a string containing a `<br>` tag — this will cause each loop to be on a new line:

```
<?php
if (isset($records)) {
  foreach ($records as $row) {
    echo $row->name.'<br>';
  }
}
```

12. Save and run this in a browser and go to `http://localhost:8000/contacts`. You will see a list of the contacts in the `contacts` table stored in the database.

Summary

In this chapter, we have gained a better understanding of the role the database class plays in the project, which is used every time the developer interacts with the database. It is a wrapper for PDO queries. They do not need to call it directly as they are extending from it.

The only library we have used is called Whoops, which will show errors in a readable format.

We have also gained experience building default states, including `baseController` and `baseMethod`.

In the next chapter, we will build a login system and authentication for users to log in and out. This will expand upon what we have covered so far and introduce new concepts. We will also be building the password recovery system in the next chapter.

7
Authentication and User Management

In the previous chapter, we have gained a better understanding of the role the `database` class plays in the project, which is used every time the developer interacts with the database.

The only library that we used is called Whoops, which will show errors in a readable format. We also gained experience building default states, including `baseController` and `baseMethod`.

In this chapter, we will be focusing on the security aspect of the project, that is, authentication. We will be building login forms which interact with the database to verify the identity of the users. Finally, we will cover how to set up a password recovery mechanism in our application.

By the end of this chapter, you will be able to:

- Build the default views for their application
- Build a password management and reset system
- Build the CRUD for a module within the system application

Setting Up Paths and Inclusion of Bootstrap

In this section, we will continue to build features on top of the framework. The core framework system files are in place. This setup is used to build useful features on top of this.

We will build the authentication system and complete the application build. Authentication is required to prevent access to unauthorized users. This ensures only the users with a valid username and password can log in to our application.

> In this chapter, we will be covering authentication. Please note that the login username and password for all the examples used in this chapter is as follows:
>
> Username: demo
>
> Password: demo

Setting up the Paths and Creating the Absolute Paths to the Files Directory

Relative paths are paths that are relative to the current folder path, for example, ./css points to a relative path one folder up and into a css folder.

Absolute paths are the full path to a file or folder, such as /user/projects/mvc/css.

This is important as this will allow files to be included using an absolute path anywhere in the framework system. This is an adaption to existing code in the system.

For example:

```
$filepath = "../app/views/$path.php";
```

This becomes:

```
$filepath = APPDIR."views/$path.php";
```

This builds on the current concept and allows views to be organized into subfolders. Without this adaptation, it will not be possible to organize anything into subfolders and it will interfere with keeping a tidy organization of code.

It is possible to continue building the system without these changes, but it is always a good idea to make sure code is tidy and organized.

Creating Layout Files

Layout files are required so that any error can be displayed.

In addition, layout files are required for the `header`, `footer`, and `navigation`. Once created, these file will provide elements that should be brought in across the application. This will include global elements.

errors.php   footer.php   header.php   nav.php

> Errors are for validation, and this is to be covered in a further subsection and not to be confused with parse errors or similar from the errors seen previously. The errors these steps are concerned with are errors related to form validation where a user inputs the incorrect information into form fields.

Inclusion of Bootstrap

Bootstrap is a HTML, CSS, and JavaScript library, and will be included for the purpose of this chapter to give a basic level of styling. It is useful for a developer as it can help them prototype and visualize how their application will look before the designer adds the design elements to an application.

In this project, Bootstrap will be included in the header as a **content delivery network (CDN)**. A CDN takes resources that are very commonly found on the web and caches them to help boost performance.

This can be easily confused with bootstrapping a framework.

Bootstrap, the HTML, CSS, and JavaScript library, and the concept of bootstrapping are two different things that share a similar name.

You can find more information on Bootstrap by visiting the following link: `https://getbootstrap.com/`.

Inclusion of Bootstrap and HTML Markup

The purpose of the section is to implement the general styling that we have implemented which shows the inclusion of bootstrap and the HTML markup:

An issue that has not yet been addressed in paths. So far, we've been using relative paths for including files such as views in `system/View.php`. Let's fix that:

1. Open `webroot/index.php` and add these lines after line 9:

```
defined('DS') || define('DS', DIRECTORY_SEPARATOR);
define('APPDIR', realpath(__DIR__.'/../app/') .DS);
define('SYSTEMDIR', realpath(__DIR__.'/../system/') .DS);
define('PUBLICDIR', realpath(__DIR__) .DS);
define('ROOTDIR', realpath(__DIR__.'/../') .DS);
```

These are constants that can be called anywhere in the framework. The first line defines a directory separator, for example, / or a \ depending on the machine:

- ° APPDIR – points to the app folder
- ° SYSTEMDIR – points to the system folder
- ° PUBLICDIR – points to the webroot folder
- ° ROOTDIR – points to the root project path

Each one creates an absolute path to its endpoint.

2. Now, let's fix the View class. Open system/View.php, and on line 24, replace:

```
$filepath = "../app/views/$path.php";
```

With:

```
$filepath = APPDIR."views/$path.php";
```

 This allows for views to include other views from parent or child folders with no issues.

3. Next, create a folder called layouts inside app/views. Create the following files inside app/views/layouts:

- ° errors.php
- ° footer.php
- ° header.php
- ° nav.php
- ° errors.php

4. Open errors.php and enter the following code:

```
<?php
use App\Helpers\Session;

if (isset($errors)) {
```

```
        foreach($errors as $error) {
            echo "<div class='alert alert-danger'>$error</div>";
        }
    }

    if (Session::get('success')) {
        echo "<div class='alert alert-success'>".
Session::pull('success')."</div>";
    }
```

This includes a Session helper, which we will create shortly.

The first if statement checks whether $errors exists, and if so, exit the loop and display an alert. The classes are Bootstrap classes (we will have this in header.php).

The next if statement checks for the existence of a session called success, and if it exists, displays its contents. This is used to provide feedback to the user.

5. Open header.php and enter the following code:

```
<!doctype html>
<html lang="en">
<head>
<meta charset="utf-8">
<title><?=(isset($title) ? $title.' - ' : '');?> Demo</
title>
<link rel="stylesheet" href="https://maxcdn.bootstrapcdn.com/
bootstrap/3.3.6/css/bootstrap.min.css">
<link rel="stylesheet" href="/css/style.css">

<script src="https://code.jquery.com/jquery-2.2.4.min.js"></
script>
<script src="https://maxcdn.bootstrapcdn.com/bootstrap/3.3.6/js/
bootstrap.min.js"></script>
</head>
<body>

<div class="container">
```

This sets the HTML document and optionally uses a $title, should it exist. Also include Bootstrap CDN CSS and JavaScript, as well as jQuery and a custom style.css file located in `webroot/css/style.css` – create this file.

6. Now, open `footer.php` and close the container `div` and the `body` and `html` tags:

For full code snippet, refer to `Lesson 7.php` file in the code files folder.

```
</div>
</body>
</html>
```

7. Now, open `nav.php` and enter the following code:

```
<nav class="navbar navbar-default">
......
        </div><!--/.nav-collapse -->
    </div><!--/.container-fluid -->
</nav>
```

This is a navigation component for Bootstrap. This is a clean way to bring in a responsive menu for our admin pages. Note the two-page links which are Admin and Users. We will also provide a logout link.

8. Now, open `app/views/404.php` and include the layout files:

```
<?php include(APPDIR.'views/layouts/header.php');?>
404!
<?php include(APPDIR.'views/layouts/footer.php');?>
```

This brings in the header and shows the page content, and ends with the footer included.

Don't include the `nav` here. The 404 can be shown even when the user is not logged in.

This makes a very clean way of organizing common layouts into your views so that when you need to change a global element, the layout views are where they were stored.

9. Open the framework in the browser if it's not already running. Run the following command from Terminal when on the root:

```
php -S localhost:8000 -t webroot
```

You won't notice anything different, but you will be redirected to a page that does not exist: `http://localhost:8000/example`.

10. You'll see a 404 page that includes the header and footer layouts. Look at the page source code – right-click and click on 'view page source'. You should see the following output:

For full code snippet, refer to `Lesson 7.php` file in the code files folder.

```
<!doctype html>
<html lang="en">
<head>
......
404!
</div>
</body>
</html>
```

These layouts will become more visible as we go further into this chapter.

In this section, we have covered how to set up file paths correctly. We covered how to set up Bootstrap properly, and we finally set up views for errors and global elements like header, footer, navigation, and errors.

In the next section, we will cover how to add security to our application and setting up a password recovery.

Adding Security to the Project

In this section, we will be continuing to build features on top of the framework. The core framework system files are in place.

The objective of this section is to build features that will add security to the project. We will be covering various aspects that we need to maintain good security in the application.

Helpers

In this subsection, we will be covering `helpers`.

We will be creating a `URL helper` and a `session helper` as well. These will be useful to authentication and indeed any other aspects of the system, but are not directly related to it.

The session helper is a `wrapper` for PHP sessions including a variety of methods useful to developers when dealing with sessions.

A `URL helper` is very similar in the sense that it is a useful method for dealing with URLs. However, in this book, it is much shorter and restricted to only a single method.

 A `session` is a way to store temporary data, like if a user is logged in or not.

Authentication

Now, we will be building the authentication functionality. Authentication is a way to allow only people with the right credentials to access restricted sections.

This will involve creating a database table and a Model:

- Creating a user's table in the database
- Create a user Model in app models
- Add insert, update delete methods

Then, we will create an admin Controller and import URL and `session` helpers as well as the `user` Model.

Lastly, we will create the associated views.

Dashboard

The project will need a dashboard; this is like a home page for a project that requires a login and normally includes links to frequently visited content for the project. In this project, we just need to make sure that the dashboard has a file that exists so that it can be directed to it. You will be creating the dashboard view and including the layout file as well as header, footer, navigation, and errors. You will be adding HTML for the page structure.

Login

The creation of the login pages also makes up part of this section.

In the login view, you will create a login form and also include the layout files.

Then, they will create a login method to handle the login process:

- Part of the process is hashing the password using password hash and bcrypt
- Use the Get data method designed to return data
- As well as creating views and the login method, we will create the `logout` method and also modify the config so that the home page, by default, will be the admin dashboard

Password Hashing

Password hashing uses bcrypt, the strongest algorithm available. Currently, the average computer would take 12 years to crack a password hash.

Part of the process is validating the data, checking if the username and passwords match what is stored in the database.

Password hashing is creating a string from your password intended to be a one-way hash, and no user should be able to determine the original content of the hash.

Password hashing is not to be confused with encryption. The difference is that in password hashing, you can decrypt the hashed password to its original state.

Implementing Validation in PHP

In this section, we'll look at getting the following outcome.

This section shows how to implement validation in PHP, although it will not work correctly yet as we are yet to create and supply the data source that forms the knowledge of the system.

To resolve this as part of the section, we will be manually creating a user.

Follow these steps to implement validation in PHP:

Creating Helpers:

1. Before we can start building the authentication, we need two new helpers. In app/Helpers, create a new file called Url.php and enter:

```php
<?php namespace App\Helpers;

class Url
{
    public static function redirect($path = '/')
    {
        header('Location: '.$path);
        exit();
    }
}
```

> This provides a single method called redirect that defaults to / when no parameters are passed. This is an easy way to redirect to another page of our application.
>
> To use the class after it's been included into a page, use:
> `Url::redirect('url/to/redirect/to')`
>
> To redirect to the home page, use:
>
> `Url::redirect()`
>
> Next, we need a way of using a session. Sessions are a way PHP can track data from page to page, which is perfect for our needs, such as being able to detect is a user is logged in or not by reading the session data.
>
> We could use normal $_SESSION calls, but since we're using OOP, let's take advantage of that and build a session helper.

2. Create a file called Session.php inside app/Helpers.

3. First, set the namespace and class definition:

The first method needed is to determine if a session has started. If it does update the `sessionStarted` parameter, it will set it to `false`. This will tell the `init` method to turn on sessions:

```php
<?php namespace App\Helpers;

class Session
{
    private static $sessionStarted = false;
    /**
     * if session has not started, start sessions
     */
    public static function init()
    {
        if (self::$sessionStarted == false) {
            session_start();
            self::$sessionStarted = true;
        }
    }
}
```

4. Next, create a method called `set` which accepts two parameters, `$key` and `$value`. This is used to add a `$key` to a session and set the `$value` to the `$key`:

```php
public static function set($key, $value = false)
{
    /**
     * Check whether session is set in array or not
     * If array then set all session key-values in foreach loop
     */
    if (is_array($key) && $value === false) {
        foreach ($key as $name => $value) {
            $_SESSION[$name] = $value;
        }
    } else {
        $_SESSION[$key] = $value;
    }
}
```

5. Next, create a method called `pull` with one parameter. This will extract the key from the session and return it after removing it from the session, which is useful for one-time messages:

```php
public static function pull($key)
{
    $value = $_SESSION[$key];
    unset($_SESSION[$key]);
    return $value;
}
```

6. Next, create a get method. This will return a session from the provided key:

```php
public static function get($key)
{
    if (isset($_SESSION[$key])) {
        return $_SESSION[$key];
    }

    return false;
}
```

> Sometimes, you want to see the contents of the session.
> Create a method called `display` that returns the `$_SESSION` object:
>
> ```php
> public static function display()
> {
>     return $_SESSION;
> }
> ```

7. The last method is used to destroy the session key when the `$key` is provided, otherwise the entire session will be destroyed:

```php
public static function destroy($key = '')
{
    if (self::$sessionStarted == true) {
        if (empty($key)) {
            session_unset();
            session_destroy();
        } else {
            unset($_SESSION[$key]);
        }
    }
}
```

The full class looks like this:

For full code snippet, refer to `Lesson 7.php` file in the code files folder.

```php
<?php namespace App\Helpers;

class Session
{
    private static $sessionStarted = false;
....
    }

}
```

8. Now, we need to set sessions automatically when the application runs. We do this by adding `Session::init()` inside `app/Config.php`:

This makes use of a `Use` Statement and includes a call to the `session's helper` class. Highlighting these OOP features may be beneficial at this stage.

For full code snippet, refer to `Lesson 7.php` file in the code files folder.

```php
<?php namespace App;

use App\Helpers\Session;

class Config {
....
        ];
    }
}
```

Building Authentication:

We are now ready to start building the admin Controller and users Model, which will be the entry point for users to log in.

1. Create a new table in your database called users:

```
CREATE TABLE `users` (
   `id` int(11) unsigned NOT NULL AUTO_INCREMENT,
   `username` varchar(255) DEFAULT NULL,
   `email` varchar(255) DEFAULT NULL,
   `password` varchar(255) DEFAULT NULL,
   `created_at` datetime DEFAULT NULL,
   `reset_token` varchar(255) DEFAULT NULL,
   PRIMARY KEY (`id`)
) ENGINE=InnoDB DEFAULT CHARSET=utf8;
```

The ID is the primary key and will be set to auto increment, meaning each record will have a unique ID.

The reset_token will only be used when a reset password procedure is needed.

2. Let's start with the Model. Create a file called User.php inside app\Models.

3. Set the namespace and import the base Model and set the class definition.

We will be coming back to this model as we go along to add necessary methods as required.

4. Add methods for inserting, updating, and deleting records:

For full code snippet, refer to `Lesson 7.php` file in the code files folder.

```php
<?php namespace App\Models;
.......
    {
        $this->db->delete('users', $where);
    }
}
```

Creation of Admin Controller:

1. Now, create a new file in `app/Controllers` called `Admin.php`.

   This will be the entry point for logging in and out of the admin dashboard.

2. Set the namespace and import the `baseController` and the `Session` and `URL` helpers as well as the `User` Model.

3. Set the class definition and create a property called `$user`. Then, in the __
   construct method, initialize the `User` Model by calling `new User()`.

 This means to access any methods of the User Model, `$this->user` can be used.

The next method is `index()`. This will load the dashboard view as long as the user is logged in.

4. To ensure that the user is logged in, an `if` statement is run to check for the existence of a session key called `logged_jn`, which is set only after logging in. If the user is not logged in, then redirect them to the `login` method:

 For full code snippet, refer to `Lesson 7.php` file in the code files folder.

```php
<?php namespace App\Controllers;

use System\BaseController;
........
        $this->view->render('admin/index', compact('title'));
    }

}
```

5. If the user is logged in, then the `admin/index` view will be loaded. Create the view `app/views/admin/index.php` and the entry:

```php
<?php
include(APPDIR.'views/layouts/header.php');
include(APPDIR.'views/layouts/nav.php');
include(APPDIR.'views/layouts/errors.php');
?>


<h1>Dashboard</h1>
<p>This is the application dashboard.</p>

<?php include(APPDIR.'views/layouts/footer.php');?>
```

Now, we need to create a `login` view. Create a folder called `auth` inside `app/views/admin` and create `login.php`.

6. First, include the `header` layout and then create a `div` with a caller of `wrapper` and `well`. The `well` class is a bootstrap class which gives a grey square styling. The `wrapper` class will be used to position the `div`.

7. Next, include the `errors` layout to catch any errors or messages.

8. Now, we'll create a form that will have a method of `post` to POST its contents to an ACTION URL, in this case, `/admin/login`.

9. Then, create two inputs for the `username` and `password`. Make sure the input type for password is set to `password`.

> Setting the input type to `password` stops the password from being displayed on the screen.
>
> When the form is submitted, the named attributes of the inputs is how PHP will know what the data is.

A submit button is also required to submit the form. A good practice is to offer a reset option if the user cannot remember their login details. We will create a link that points the user to `/admin/reset`.

10. Finally, close the form and include the footer layout:

> For full code snippet, refer to `Lesson 7.php` file in the code files folder.

```php
<?php include(APPDIR.'views/layouts/header.php');?>

<div class="wrapper well">

    <?php include(APPDIR.'views/layouts/errors.php');?>
```
....
```css
.wrapper h1 {
    margin-top: 0px;
    font-size: 25px;
}
```

11. Now, go back to the admin Controller and create a `login` method:

 Put in a check that redirects the user if they are logged in. They should not be able to see the login page when they are already logged in.

12. Inside the `login` method, create an empty `$errors` array and set the page `$title` and load a view calling `admin/auth/login`, passing the `$title` and `$errors` variables by using a `compact` function.

> `compact()` makes it possible to use variables by simply entering their names without the `$`:
>
> ```php
> public function login()
> {
>     if (Session::get('logged_in')) {
>         Url::redirect('/admin');
>     }
>
>     $errors = [];
>
>     $title = 'Login';
>
>     $this->view->render('admin/auth/login',
> compact('title', 'errors'));
> }
> ```

This loads the `login` view and, upon pressing submit, won't actually do anything. We'll need to check for the form being submitted, but before doing that, we will need to add two methods to the `user` Model:

```
public function get_hash($username)
{
    $data = $this->db->select('password FROM users WHERE username
= :username', [':username' => $username]);
    return (isset($data[0]->password) ? $data[0]->password : null);
}
```

`get_hash($username)` will select the `password` from the `users` table, where the `username` matches the one provided.

Setting `username = :username` creates a placeholder. Then, `[':username' => $username]` will use that placeholder so it knows what the value is going to be.

Then, check whether `$data[0]->password` is set and return it. Otherwise, return `null`.

13. Do the same thing again for `get_data()`, only this time, return an array of data rather than a single column:

```
public function get_data($username)
{
    $data = $this->db->select('* FROM users WHERE username =
:username', [':username' => $username]);
    return (isset($data[0]) ? $data[0] : null);
}
```

14. Now, inside our `login` method, we can check whether the form has been submitted by checking if the `$_POST` array contains an object called `submit`.

15. Then, collect the form data and store them on local variables. Using `htmlspecialchars()` is a security measure, since it stops script tags from being able to be executed and renders them as plaintext.

Next, an `if` statement is run that calls `password_verify()`, which is a built-in function which returns `true` or `false`. The first parameter is the user-provided `$password`, and the second is the hashed password returned from the database by calling `$this->user->get_hash($username)`. As long as `password_verify` equals to `false`, the login check has failed.

16. Set an `$errors` variable to contain an `errors` message. Next, count the `$errors` and if it equals to `0`, this means there are no errors so get the user data from `$this->user->get_data($username)`. Then, use the session helper to create a session key called `logged_in` with a value of `true`, and another session key with the user ID as its value.

17. Finally, redirect the user to the admin `index` page:

```
if (isset($_POST['submit'])) {
        $username = htmlspecialchars($_POST['username']);
        $password = htmlspecialchars($_POST['password']);
        if (password_verify($password, $this->user->get_
hash($username)) == false) {
            $errors[] = 'Wrong username or password';
        }
        if (count($errors) == 0) {
            //logged in
            $data = $this->user->get_data($username);
            Session::set('logged_in', true);
            Session::set('user_id', $data->id);

            Url::redirect('/admin');
        }
    }
```

The full method looks like this:

```
public function login()
{
    if (Session::get('logged_in')) {
        Url::redirect('/admin');
    }
......
    $this->view->render('admin/auth/login', compact('title',
'errors'));
}
```

18. Run the framework if it's not already running:

```
php -S localhost:8000 -t webroot
```

19. Go to `http://localhost:8000/admin/login`.

You will see a login page. Pressing login will show an error message of 'Wrong username or password' no matter what you enter, as there are currently no users in the database.

20. Let's create our login. We need a hashed password to store in the database. To create one in the `login` method, enter:

```
echo password_hash('demo', PASSWORD_BCRYPT);
```

The first parameter is the `password` you want, in this case, `demo`. The second parameter is the type of `PASSWORD` function to use. Using the default `PASSWORD_ BCRYPT` means PHP will use the strongest version possible.

21. When you refresh the page, you will see a hash like the following:

```
$2y$10$OAZK6znqAvV2fXS1BbYoVet3pC9dStWVFQGlrgEV4oz2
GwJi0nKtC
```

22. Copy this and insert a new record into the database client and leave the ID column blank. That will populate itself.

23. Create a `username` and `email` and paste them into the `hash`. For the password, enter a valid `datetime` for the `created at` section, such as 2017-12-04 23:04:00.

24. Save the record. Now, you will be able to set up the login.

25. Upon logging in, you'll be redirected to `/admin`.

 Remember to comment out or remove `echo password_ hash('demo', PASSWORD_BCRYPT)`, otherwise the hash will always be displayed.

26. While we're at it, let's go ahead and add in the ability to log out. Logging out is a case of destroying the logged-in and `user_id` sessions. In the `Admin Controller`, create a new method called `logout`.

27. Inside the method, destroy the session `object` and then redirect to the `login` page:

```
public function logout()
{
    Session::destroy();
    Url::redirect('/admin/login');
}
```

28. Now, go back to the application and click `logout` in the upper-right corner. You will be logged out and taken back to the `login` page.

29. Now, log back in. If you click on the `Admin` link, you will be taken to the default page. In this case, it would be better to load the admin as soon as you load the application. We can do this by setting the `Admin` Controller to be the default `app/Config.php`.

    Find the following:

    ```
    'default_controller' => 'Home'
    ```

    Replace it with:

    ```
    'default_controller' => Admin,
    ```

30. Now, if you click on `Admin` (after reloading the page), you'll see the admin dashboard.

> There was once a time where certain standards for password hashing were considered to be the highest level of internet security. But, like most technology, it is inevitably made available, and this weakens the effectiveness of its predecessors.

> Avoid the following hashing systems at all costs as they are not secure:
> - MD5
> - Shar 1
> - Shar 2 56
>
> These password hashing functions are weak, and computers are now so powerful that it would take just seconds to break them.
>
> It is advisable to comb through code when a developer is scoping out a new project to check for security flaws like the use of these.

In this section, we learned about the authentication process. We have seen how to make a login process. We have learned the process of password hashing. Now, we have experience in building, configuring, and routing functionality to a framework.

In the next section, we will cover the concept of password recovery wherein we will set up a functionality to reset the password in our application.

Password Recovery

This section is all about setting up the ability to reset the password. Password resets are very crucial because there might be a case where users forget their passwords. We will now build a password recovery process, similar to the following image:

Generic password recovery example found on the web

We will create a method called reset in the admin Controller. This process loads up a view where the users will enter their email address to request an email. When this is processed, this will validate to make sure that the email address is valid and actually exists on the system.

This will check against the email, ensuring that it is in the right format, and will check that the email address provided exists in the database table named users.

Introduction to a Third-Party Dependency PHP Mailer

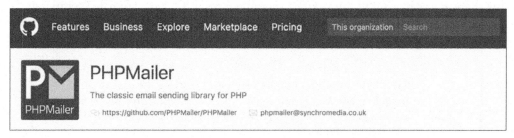

Image from PHP Mailer: https://github.com/PHPMailer

We are going to add a third-party dependency by including PHP Mailer for sending out emails.

PHP Mailer works like this:

1. Provided that the validation had passed, we will then use PHP Mailer to send an email with a token. The token will later be received over email and entered into a hidden field as part of a form, fulfilling a requirement for the validation process.

 A token is simply a random string of letters and numbers. The idea is to generate something unique for that user to identify that the request is coming from them.

2. The next part of the process is to send an email to the user, and when the user clicks on this, create a method to process that request. This involves creating a change password method that accepts the token provided by the email, which then displays the view with the form inside it.

3. Next, in the view, the token is resent in a hidden field. Additionally, users can enter a new password and confirm this password. When submitted, the Controller will process the data and validate it. This involves ensuring the token matches the user account and that the password is long enough and that both passwords match.

4. After creating this, when the update is put into practice, the users will be able to log in to the admin system automatically without having to re-enter their password.

This saves users having to log in once they have reset their password. Technically, this is a user experience design update, although you can see here that UX changes are not just restricted to the designer realm.

> PHP Mailer checks that the format is correct. In the case of an email, this will be expecting that the @ symbol is present. This is just one example of a validation check. PHP has methods built in so that it can determine that the correct format is a valid format.

Building a Password Reset Mechanism for Our Application

To complete the authentication system, we need the ability to reset the password should we forget what it is. Here are the steps to do so:

1. Create a new method called `reset` in the `Admin` Controller.

2. Again, check if the user is logged in and if they are, redirect them back to the admin.

3. Set up an `errors` array and set the page title before loading a view called `reset`:

```php
public function reset()
{
    if (Session::get('logged_in')) {
        Url::redirect('/admin');
    }

    $errors = [];

    $title = 'Reset Account';

    $this->view->render('admin/auth/reset', compact('title',
'errors'));
}
```

4. Now create a view called `reset.php` in `app/views/admin/auth` and enter:

```php
<?php include(APPDIR.'views/layouts/header.php');?>

<div class="wrapper well">

    <?php include(APPDIR.'views/layouts/errors.php');?>

    <h1>Reset Account</h1>

    <form method="post">
...
...
    </div>

<?php include(APPDIR.'views/layouts/footer.php');?>
```

 The form will post to the same `url` `/admin/reset`. The only data we're collecting is the email address. The email address will be used to verify that the user exists before proceeding.

5. Now, go back to the reset method on the `Admin` Controller.

6. First, check if the form has been submitted with an `isset` and pass in the submit button name:

```php
if (isset($_POST['submit'])) {
```

7. Next, make sure that the email address is `isset`, otherwise default to `null`. Check that the email address is in the correct format:

```php
$email = (isset($_POST['email']) ? $_POST['email'] : null);

if (!filter_var($email, FILTER_VALIDATE_EMAIL)) {

    $errors[] = 'Please enter a valid email address';
} else {
    if ($email != $this->user->get_user_email($email)){
        $errors[] = 'Email address not found';
    }
}
```

8. Lastly, check if the email address belongs to an existing user. To do this, create a new method in the user Model called `get_user_email($email)`:

 This will return the email address if it exists, otherwise `null` will be returned.

```php
public function get_user_email($email)
{
    $data = $this->db->select('email from users where email =
:email', [':email' => $email]);
    return (isset($data[0]->email) ? $data[0]->email : null);
}
```

In the preceding Controller, we have:

```php
if ($email != $this->user->get_user_email($email)){
```

 This checks that the email address provided in the form does not match with the database, in which case a new error is created.

9. After the validation check, there are no errors:

```php
if (count($errors) == 0) {
```

10. Save the file; the method so far looks like this:

 For full code snippet, refer to `Lesson 7.php` file in the code files folder.

```php
public function reset()
{
.......

    $this->view->render('admin/auth/reset', compact('title',
'errors'));
}
```

At this point, among other things, an email needs to be sent.

A best practice is to not use PHP's built-in `mail()` function and to use a library such as `phpmailer` (`https://github.com/PHPMailer/`) instead.

11. Open `composer.json` and `phpmailer` in the require list:

```
{
    "autoload": {
        "psr-4": {
            "App\\" : "app/",
            "System\\" : "system/"
        }
    },
    "require": {
        "filp/whoops": "^2.1",
        "phpmailer/phpmailer": "~6.0"
    }
}
```

12. Save the file and type `composer update` in Terminal. This will pull in `phpmailer`, making it available to our application.

13. At the top of the `Admin` Controller, import `phpmailer`:

```
use PHPMailer\PHPMailer\PHPMailer;
use PHPMailer\PHPMailer\Exception;
```

14. Next, go to the `reset` method inside the following `if` statement. This is where we'll resume:

```
if (count($errors) == 0) {


}
```

15. Now, we need to make a random token. For this, use `md5`, `uniqid`, and `rand` to make a random token.

16. Then, set up a `data` and `where` array. The `$data` will specify the `reset_token` to have a value of `$token`, and the `$where` will be the email address. Pass them to the `update()` method of the user Model to update the user.

    This will store the `$token` against the users record in the database:

```
$token = md5(uniqid(rand(),true));
$data  = ['reset_token' => $token];
$where = ['email' => $email];
$this->user->update($data, $where);
```

17. Now, we set up the email to be sent by creating a new instance of `phpmailer`, and then setting who the email will come from. Change this as desired.

18. Pass the `$email` address that this is going to be sent to and set the mode to HTML by passing true to isHTML():

```
$mail = new PHPMailer(true);
$mail->setFrom('noreply@domain.com');
$mail->addAddress($email);
$mail->isHTML(true);
```

19. Set the subject and the email body. We provide two bodies: a HTML one and a plaintext one. The plain text one is used in case the user's email client cannot render HTML.

20. Create a link that points to `admin/change/password_token` when using `localhost`:

 It's important to remember the URL `http://localhost:8000` will only work for your machine.

```
$mail->Subject = 'Reset you account';
$mail->Body    = "<p>To change your password please click <a
href='http://localhost:8000/admin/change_password/$token'>this
link</a></p>";
$mail->AltBody = "To change your password please go to this
address: http://localhost:8000/admin/change_password/$token";
```

21. Now, everything is set up. Send the email:

```
$mail->send();
```

22. Create a session to inform the user and redirect the admin/reset:

```
Session::set('success', "Email sent to ".htmlentities($email));
Url::redirect('/admin/reset');
```

The completed method looks like this:

 For full code snippet, refer to `Lesson 7.php` file in the code files folder.

```
public function reset()
{
    if (Session::get('logged_in')) {
        Url::redirect('/admin');
    }
....... .
    $title = 'Reset Account';

    $this->view->render('admin/auth/reset', compact('title',
'errors'));
}
```

23. When the user clicks on the link in the email, we need to handle the request.
To do this, create another method called change_password that accepts a
parameter called $token:

> This method takes the $token, passes it to a method in the users
> Model called get_user_reset_token($token), and returns
> the user object. If the token does not match the database, then null
> is returned.
>
> For full code snippet, refer to Lesson 7.php file in the code files
> folder.

```
$user = $this->user->get_user_reset_token($token);
if ($user == null) {
        $errors[] = 'user not found.';
}
```

The method looks like this:

> For full code snippet, refer to Lesson 7.php file in
> the code files folder.

```
$title = 'Change Password';

    $this->view->render('admin/auth/change_password',
compact('title', 'token', 'errors'));
}
```

> The render method passed the $title, $token, and $errors to the view.

24. Another view is needed. Create a view called change_password.php in app/ views/admin/auth:

> For full code snippet, refer to Lesson 7.php file in the code files folder.

```php
<?php include(APPDIR.'views/layouts/header.php');?>
```

......

```
    </div>
```

```php
<?php include(APPDIR.'views/layouts/footer.php');?>
```

> The form has a hidden input called $token. Its value is the $token passed from the Controller, and this will be used to verify the request.
>
> There's also two inputs: a password and confirm password. These are used to collect the desired password.
>
> When the form is submitted and the form data is collected, a method called to get_user_reset_token($token) is made again to verify that the provided token is valid.
>
> Also, the passwords must match and be more than three characters in length.

25. If there is no error, then update the user's record in the database by passing to $this->user->update an array to clear out the reset_token. Hash the password using password_hash(), where the ID matches the user object and the token matches the provided token:

> For full code snippet, refer to Lesson 7.php file in the code files folder.

```
if (isset($_POST['submit'])) {

    $token = htmlspecialchars($_POST['token']);
.......
    }


}
```

26. After the update, log the user in and redirect them to the admin dashboard.

The full method looks like this:

 For full code snippet, refer to `Lesson 7.php` file in the code files folder.

```
public function change_password($token)
{
.......

    $title = 'Change Password';

    $this->view->render('admin/auth/change_password',
compact('title', 'token', 'errors'));
    }
```

This concludes the authentication sections. We can now log in, log out, and reset the password, should we forget it.

We have now come to the end of this section. Here, we learned how to build a password reset system and also gained further experience in using third-party tools.

In the next section, we will see how to add CRUD functionality for user management.

Building CRUD for User Management

CRUD

The users section allows for the creation and management of users of the application built on top of the framework.

We will create the CRUD to enable:

- Creation of users
- Display of existing users
- Update of existing users
- Deletion of unwanted users

In this section, we will be creating the different methods in the users Controller.

We will also be creating more methods in the users Model for the new queries that will be required to retrieve all users or to retrieve a specific user.

The process will be as follows:

1. Part of this process is to create a construct method, which allows us to secure all methods from unauthorized users. This means that to be able to access any method within the section, you must be logged in first. The index method lists all the users with options to edit and delete the user.

2. On delete, a confirmation will be presented first.

3. The next step is to create an add view. In this view, there will be the form for the users of the application to create their record of a new user for the application. On submission of the form, the data will be collected and the validation process will start.

4. This will check that the data that is submitted is appropriate for its purpose and likely to be what is expected.

   For example, there will be a check making sure that the username is more than three characters in length and does not already exist in the database.

    This process is the same for the email, and in the case of the email, it is making sure it is valid and does not exist already.

5. After the validation is passed, the user is created and a success message is recorded and visible to the user. The application user is then redirected to the users view.

6. We will then create an `update` method and `view`, which is much like the method and view for creating a user. The key difference is that the form is pre-populated with the user's details upon being loaded onto the page, and when the form is submitted, that particular user is updated rather than a new record being created.

7. The final method to be made is the `delete` method, which checks that the ID of the user is numeric and is not the same as the ID for the logged-in user so that they cannot delete themselves.

This is a case of the developer underestimating what a user might do. It is surprising what a user may do intentionally or unintentionally, and cases where they may delete themselves is easily done if the application takes no steps to prevent this.

After the record is deleted, a success message is created, and the user is redirected back to the user's page.

Building CRUD for User Management

In this section, we'll look at having the following output displayed on our screen:

> When reading a user, know that in this table it is possible to control what is displayed. Not all information about that user needs to be displayed.
>
> In this section, we will build our users section to Create, Read, Update, and Delete users.

Follow these steps to build CRUD for user management:

1. First, we need a few more queries. Open app/Models/User.php.

2. Create the following methods:

> For full code snippet, refer to Lesson 7.php file in the code files folder.

```
get_users() - returns all users ordered by username
    $data = $this->db->select('username from users where username
= :username', [':username' => $username]);
    return (isset($data[0]->username) ? $data[0]->username :
null);
}
```

3. Now, create a Users Controller in app/Controllers. Create Users.php.

4. Set the namespace and import the helpers and User Model:

```
<?php namespace App\Controllers;
```

```
use System\BaseController;
use App\Helpers\Session;
use App\Helpers\Url;
use App\Models\User;
class Users extends BaseController
{
```

5. Next, create a class property called $user and a __construct method. Then, check if the user is logged in, and if not, redirect them to the login page.

6. Create a new user instance:

```
$this->user = new User()
```

Doing this check in a construct means all the methods of this class will be protected from unauthorized users.

```php
protected $user;

public function __construct()
{
    parent::__construct();

    if (! Session::get('logged_in')) {
        Url::redirect('/admin/login');
    }

    $this->user = new User();
}
```

7. Next, create an index method. This will call `get_users()` and load a view and pass in the users object:

```php
public function index()
{
    $users = $this->user->get_users();
    $title = 'Users';

    $this->view->render('admin/users/index', compact('users',
'title'));
}
```

8. For the view, create `app/views/admin/users/index.php`.

9. Include the layout files and create a table to display a list of users:

```php
foreach($users as $user)
```

10. Loop through all the user records. As a security measure, when printing data from a database, we'll make use of `htmlentities()`. This converts all tags into their HTML counterparts, meaning if any code had been injected into the database, it would simply be printed as text, making it useless:

For full code snippet, refer to `Lesson 7.php` file in the code files folder.

```php
<?php
include(APPDIR.'views/layouts/header.php');
include(APPDIR.'views/layouts/nav.php');
......
    </table>
</div>

<?php include(APPDIR.'views/layouts/footer.php');?>
```

11. Inside the loop, we have two action links for editing and deleting. Note that the user's ID is being passed to the end of the `href` value. This is to pass the ID to the URL.

12. Also, we have an `Add User` button that points to /users/add. Let's create this. In your `Users` Controller, create a new method called `add()`:

```php
public function add()
    {
        $errors = [];

        $title = 'Add User';
        $this->view->render('admin/users/add', compact('errors',
'title'));
    }
```

13. Now, create a view in `app/views/admin/users` called `add.php`.

14. Include the layout files and set the page title. Next, create a form with a method set to `post`.

15. You need four inputs for `username`, `email`, `password`, and `confirm password`. Make sure each input has a name.

> Sticky forms is useful in the event of errors.
>
> Sticky forms are forms that retain their data in the event of an error. The inputs will still show the values entered into them.

16. To implement sticky forms on the username and email, use a ternary:

```php
(isset($_POST['username']) ? $_POST['username'] : '')
```

This says if the `$_POST['username']` is set, then print it, otherwise print an empty string:

For full code snippet, refer to `Lesson 7.php` file in the code files folder.

```php
<?php
include(APPDIR.'views/layouts/header.php');
include(APPDIR.'views/layouts/nav.php');
include(APPDIR.'views/layouts/errors.php');
........
</form>

<?php include(APPDIR.'views/layouts/footer.php');?>
```

17. When submitted, the form data will be posted to `/users/add`. This needs handling in the `add` method of the `Users` Controller.

18. Check for the form submission:

```php
if (isset($_POST['submit'])) {
```

19. Next, collect the form data:

```php
$username          = (isset($_POST['username']) ? $_
POST['username'] : null);
$email             = (isset($_POST['email']) ? $_
POST['email'] : null);
$password          = (isset($_POST['password']) ? $_
POST['password'] : null);
$password_confirm  = (isset($_POST['password_confirm']) ? $_
POST['password_confirm'] : null);
```

20. Then, start the validation process.

21. Check that the `username` is more than 3 characters in length:

```php
if (strlen($username) < 3) {
    $errors[] = 'Username is too short';
}
```

22. Next, check if the $username exists already in the database by passing $username to a get_user_username($username) method on the Model. If the results are the same as $username, then it already exists, so create an error:

```
else {
    if ($username == $this->user->get_user_username($username)){
        $errors[] = 'Username address is already in use';
    }
}
```

23. For email validation, check that the email is in a valid format by using filter_var and FILTER_VALIDATE_EMAIL. If this does not return true, create an error.

24. Like with the username, check if the $email exists in the database already:

```
if (!filter_var($email, FILTER_VALIDATE_EMAIL)) {
    $errors[] = 'Please enter a valid email address';
} else {
    if ($email == $this->user->get_user_email($email)){
        $errors[] = 'Email address is already in use';
    }
}
```

25. For the passwords, check that $password matches $password_confirm or creates an error. Otherwise, check that the password is more than 3 characters in length:

```
if ($password != $password_confirm) {
    $errors[] = 'Passwords do not match';
} elseif (strlen($password) < 3) {
    $errors[] = 'Password is too short';
}
```

26. If there are no errors, carry on and set a $data array containing the data to be inserted into the database.

 Note the password using a password_hash() function. This is using PHP's built-in password function that, by default, will use bcrypt, which at the time of writing is the most secure hashing technique.

27. Create the user by calling `$this->insert($data)` and set a message before redirecting back to /users:

```
if (count($errors) == 0) {

    $data = [
        'username' => $username,
        'email' => $email,
        'password' => password_hash($password, PASSWORD_BCRYPT)
    ];

    $this->user->insert($data);

    Session::set('success', 'User created');
    Url::redirect('/users');


}
```

The full method looks like this:

 For full code snippet, refer to `Lesson 7.php` file in the code files folder.

```
public function add()
    {
        $errors = [];
.......
        $title = 'Add User';
        $this->view->render('admin/users/add', compact('errors',
'title'));
    }
```

28. To edit users, the URL structure is /users/edit/1. The number at the end is the ID of the user.

29. Create a method called `edit($id)` that accepts a parameter called `$id`.

30. First, check that `$id` is a number, otherwise redirect back to /users.

31. Get the user's data by calling `$this>user->get_user($id)` and pass in the ID to the `users` Model method. This will return a `user` object or `null` if the record is not found.

32. If the `$user` is equal to `null`, redirect to a `404` page. Otherwise, set up an `$errors` array, `$title`, and load the view, passing in user, errors, and title to `compact()`:

```php
public function edit($id)
{
    if (! is_numeric($id)) {
  Url::redirect('/users');
    }
    $user = $this->user->get_user($id);
    if ($user == null) {
        Url::redirect('/404');
    }

    $errors = [];

    $title = 'Edit User';
    $this->view->render('admin/users/edit', compact('user',
'errors', 'title'));
}
```

33. Now, create a view in `app/views/admin/users` called `edit.php`:

This is almost identical to the `add.php` view. The main difference is in the username and email inputs. They are pre-populated with the user object:

```
<input class="form-control" id="username" type="text"
name="username" value="<?=$user->username;?>" required />
```

The `<?=$user->username;?>` is the user object in action using `->` after `$user`. You specify what column you want out of it.

It's important that you do not pre-populate the password fields; they should only be filled in when the user wants to change the password. As such, put a message to inform the user that they should enter the password only if they want to change their existing password:

For full code snippet, refer to `Lesson 7.php` file in the code files folder.

```php
<?php
include(APPDIR.'views/layouts/header.php');
include(APPDIR.'views/layouts/nav.php');
include(APPDIR.'views/layouts/errors.php');
......
</form>

<?php include(APPDIR.'views/layouts/footer.php');?>
```

When this is submitted, the `edit($id)` method will process the request.

34. Just like the `add()` method, check for the form submission, collect the form data, and perfect the form validation.

35. This time, we won't check if the username or email exists in the database, only that they are provided and are valid:

For full code snippet, refer to `Lesson 7.php` file in the code files folder.

```php
if (isset($_POST['submit'])) {
    $username                = (isset($_POST['username']) ? $_
POST['username'] : null);
......
            $errors[] = 'Password is too short';
        }
    }
```

36. Next, check that there are no errors:

```
if (count($errors) == 0) {
```

37. Set the `$data` array to update the user's record. This time, only the username and email are provided:

```
$data = [
    'username' => $username,
    'email' => $email
];
```

38. If the password has been updated, then add the password to the `$data` array:

```
if ($password != null) {
    $data['password'] = password_hash($password, PASSWORD_BCRYPT);
}
```

39. The where statement says where the ID matches `$id`. Run the `update()` and set a message and redirect to the users page:

```
$where = ['id' => $id];

$this->user->update($data, $where);

Session::set('success', 'User updated');

Url::redirect('/users');
```

The full `update` method looks like this:

 For full code snippet, refer to `Lesson 7.php` file in the code files folder.

```
public function edit($id)
{
    if (! is_numeric($id)) {
......
    }
    $title = 'Edit User';
    $this->view->render('admin/users/edit', compact('user',
'errors', 'title'));
}
```

40. The last step to complete the users Controller is adding the ability to delete users.

41. Like the edit, the URL structure will pass in an `$id` as part of the URL in the format of `/users/delete/2`.

42. Create a method called `delete($id)`.

43. Check if the `$id` is numeric and check if the `$id` matches the session `$_SESSION['user_id']`, otherwise kill the page. You don't want to allow a user to delete their own record.

44. Next, get the user by calling `$this->user->get_user($id)` and check if the `$user` object is not equal to `null`. Otherwise, redirect to a `404` page.

45. Next, create a `$where` array that says where the `$id` matches the ID in the database. Note we do not use a `$data` array. In this case, we only pass a `$where`. This is because you cannot select columns, only a row, so the `$data` would be pointless.

46. Lastly, set a message and redirect back to `/users`:

```
public function delete($id)
    {
        if (! is_numeric($id)) {
            Url::redirect('/users');
        }
        if (Session::get('user_id') == $id) {
            die('You cannot delete yourself.');
        }
        $user = $this->user->get_user($id);
        if ($user == null) {
            Url::redirect('/404');
        }
        $where = ['id' => $user->id];
        $this->user->delete($where);
        Session::set('success', 'User deleted');
        Url::redirect('/users');
    }
```

47. Now, run the application:

```
php -S localhost:8000 -t webroot
```

48. Go to `http://localhost:8000/users`, click on `Add User`, and fill in the form.

49. First, if you try to submit the form without any data, you will see the HTML client validation that comes from putting a required attribute on the inputs.

50. Try filling in a user with the same username as one you've already created, and you'll see the server validation rules up and running.

51. Finally, fill in the form completely with new user details and you will be redirected to `/users` and see the new user, along with a confirmation message.

52. Click on `Edit` next to the user you want to edit. You will then be presented with the edit form with the username and email filled in. Pressing submit will take you back to the users page.

53. Pressing `delete` will delete the user right away (providing the user is not you) with no confirmation. Let's fix that!

54. Our requirement states that when the user presses `delete`, a confirmation window should be displayed. If OK is clicked, then the delete URL will be called, and if cancel is clicked, nothing will happen.

55. Open `app/views/admin/users/index.php` and place this JavaScript before the `footer.php` code block:

```
<script language="JavaScript" type="text/javascript">
function del(id, title) {
    if (confirm("Are you sure you want to delete '" + title +
"'?")) {
        window.location.href = '/users/delete/' + id;
    }
}
</script>
```

56. This defines a JavaScript function which accepts an ID and a `username`. When the `confirm()` passes a `window.location.href`, it will run, redirecting the page to the delete URL before passing in the ID `var` to the end of the URL.

57. In the loop where you see the delete link:

```
<a href="/users/delete/<?=$row->id;?>" class="btn btn-xs btn-
danger">Delete</a>
```

Replace it with:

```
<a href="javascript:del('<?=$row->id;?>','<?=$row->username;?>')"
class="btn btn-xs btn-danger">Delete</a>
```

This calls `javascript:del()`, which triggers the confirmation popup and passes in the user's `ID` and `username`.

58. Save the file and run the page. When you click on delete, you will now see a confirmation prompt. Clicking OK will allow the delete to go ahead, while pressing cancel will stop the redirect from running.

Optional Activity

1. Add additional fields about a user, perhaps their address, age, hobbies, eye color, or anything of your, choosing.

2. Ensure these are processed in the `Method` and `Controller` and ensure that the database table is ready to accept them.

3. Ensure that these are included in the view.

4. In the `index` view, the student can select information of their choosing to help identify the user in the table.

Summary

In this chapter, we have completed building functionality onto the framework, which allows for the management of users. We have performed the inclusion of Bootstrap to give some basic-level styling to our application. We have also implemented a password recovery mechanism in our application.

This completes the most basic requirements of the contacts application. However, all of this involves the ability to log in to an area containing the application, which is restricted without the correct username and password credentials. This is, at the moment, just an empty dashboard page. With everything in place, we can now move on to building the application to store the user's contacts.

In the next chapter, we will look at how to build a contacts management system on top of our current application which will include creating, reading, updating, deleting, and using a contact in the contacts application.

8
Building a Contacts Management System

In the previous chapter, we have completed building functionality onto the framework, which allows for the management of users. We have performed the inclusion of Bootstrap to give some basic-level styling to our application. We have also implemented a password recovery mechanism in our application.

In this chapter, we will build a contacts CRUD (Create, Read, Update, and Delete) section, which will have a view page to view an individual contact. The view page comments can be recorded against the contact. We will also be building the comments system for our contact application.

By the end of this chapter, you will be able to:

- Implement CRUD functionality in our contacts application
- Build a comments system in our contacts application

Overview CMS

A framework is an abstraction in software which provides multiple software that can be used by writing custom user code. The flow of control in a framework is not decided like in other libraries:

The dashboard of the application

Here is the dashboard — the page users land on when logging in. From here, they can navigate to the section of the application where they will be able to manage content:

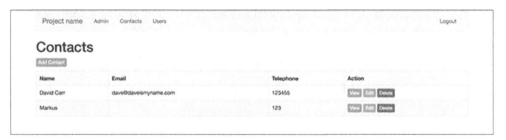

The contacts index page

This is the `contacts` index, where users view all of the contacts stored in the contacts table.

This is the knowledge of the application built on top of the framework.

The user can see the name of the contact as well as the email address address and telephone number related to each contact.

The user is unable to see the contact ID, but this ID is still generated, and forms part of the URL for the view, edit, and delete; so, when a functionality is triggered by clicking on one of these buttons, it already knows which record in the contacts table to draw its knowledge from.

Viewing an individual contact

This is the contact page.

This page displays all of the information in a single record. The record in this application is the data of a unique contact, which is represented by an ID. The ID is unique, so only the information of one single contact will ever be displayed:

Caution

The word unique here is used because it is a separate ID. If it is stored as a separate ID, then it is considered a unique record by the application.

The add contact page

This is the page where the form is displayed which allows a user to add a completely new contact.

This page, when loading, requires no parameters as it does not need to load any pre-populated data in its fields.

When submitting, assuming there are no errors, a new contact will be added:

The edit contact page

This is the page where a form is displayed which allows a user to edit a contact.

The difference in this page is that the data stored in relation to a contact record is pre-populated in the form.

The reason it is possible to do this is that the edit page is loaded with the contact ID passed as a parameter. This ID tells the system which record it should be loading into this page.

CRUD, the Contact Application

In this section, users will create the functionality to CRUD the contact application. Users will:

- Create new contact records
- View all the contact records
- View individual contact records
- Update the contact records
- Delete the contact records

You may find this very similar to building the user management functionality and would be right to do so.

CRUD lies at the heart of all applications, and functionality is extended from there.

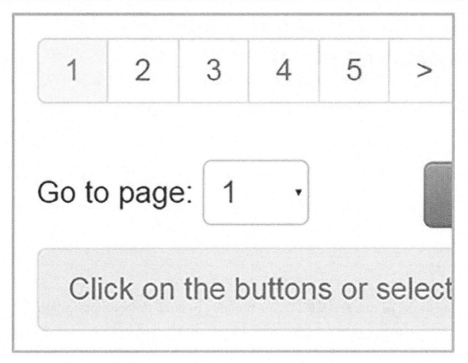

This is an example of pagination

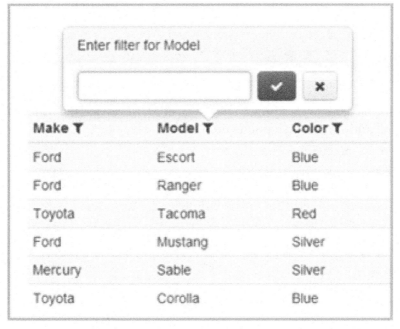

This is an example of filtering

Inserting CRUD functionality in Our Contacts Application

In this section, we'll try to insert CRUD functionality in our Contacts application.

Have a look at the following screenshot:

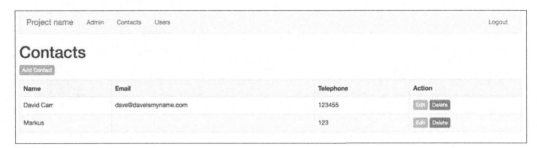

The outcome of this section

Here are the steps to insert CRUD functionality in our Contacts application:

1. In the database, we need a `contacts` table (remove one if you have it from earlier chapters):

```
CREATE TABLE `contacts` (
    `id` int(11) unsigned NOT NULL AUTO_INCREMENT,
    `name` varchar(255) DEFAULT NULL,
    `email` varchar(255) DEFAULT NULL,
    `tel` varchar(255) DEFAULT NULL,
    PRIMARY KEY (`id`)
) ENGINE=InnoDB AUTO_INCREMENT=4 DEFAULT CHARSET=utf8;
```

2. The `contacts` table stores a unique ID of each contact, the contact's name, email address, and telephone number.

3. Next, we need a `comments` table:

```
CREATE TABLE `comments` (
    `id` int(11) unsigned NOT NULL AUTO_INCREMENT,
    `contact_id` int(11) DEFAULT NULL,
    `user_id` int(11) DEFAULT NULL,
    `body` text,
    `created_at` timestamp NULL DEFAULT CURRENT_TIMESTAMP,
    PRIMARY KEY (`id`)
) ENGINE=InnoDB AUTO_INCREMENT=3 DEFAULT CHARSET=utf8;
```

The comments must have the `contact_id` and `user_id` fields. These are foreign keys to link a comment back to a contact and a user who posted the comment.

The comment will be added to the body field, and a `created_at` column is used to note when a record was created. This column is set with a timestamp with a default `CURRENT_TIMESTAMP`. This means the date and time will automatically be inserted when a new record is added:

4. Since we've experimented with contacts in earlier chapters, let's start by doing some cleanups. Delete the `app/views/contacts` folder.

5. Open `app/views/layouts/nav.php` and add a contacts menu item that points to `/contacts`:

```
<nav class="navbar navbar-default">
    <div class="container-fluid">
....... .
    </div><!--/.container-fluid -->
</nav>
```

6. Open `app/Models/Contacts.php`.

7. Remove this code:

```
public function getContacts()
{
    return $this->db->select('* FROM contacts');
}
```

Then, replace it with this:

```
public function get_contacts()
{
    return $this->db->select('* from contacts order by name');
}
```

8. Next, we need a method to load a single contact, where the ID belongs to the contact:

```
public function get_contact($id)
{
    $data = $this->db->select('* from contacts where id = :id',
[':id' => $id]);
    return (isset($data[0]) ? $data[0] : null);
}
```

9. We will also need `insert`, `update`, and `delete` methods:

```php
public function insert($data)
{
    $this->db->insert('contacts', $data);
}
public function update($data, $where)
{
    $this->db->update('contacts', $data, $where);
}
public function delete($where)
{
    $this->db->delete('contacts', $where);
}
```

The full model looks like this:

 For full code snippet, refer to `Lesson 8.php` file in the code files folder.

```php
<?php
namespace App\Models;

use System\BaseModel;

class Contact extends BaseModel
......
    }
}
```

10. Next, open `app/Controllers/Contacts.php`.

11. Import the `Session` and URL helpers:

```php
Use App\Helpers\Session;
Use App\Helpers\Url;
```

12. Replace the following code:

```php
public function index()
{
  $contacts = new Contact();
    $records = $contacts->getContacts();
```

```
    return $this->view->render('contacts/index',
compact('records'));
}
```

With this:

```
protected $contact;
public function __construct()
{
    parent::__construct();
    if (! Session::get('logged_in')) {
        Url::redirect('/admin/login');
    }
    $this->contact = new Contact();
}
public function index()
{
    $contacts = $this->contact->get_contacts();
    $title = 'Contacts';
    return $this->view->render('admin/contacts/index',
compact('contacts', 'title'));
}
```

Like our Users controller, this will ensure you are logged in before being able to access the contacts, and sets up the $contact model, collecting the contacts and loading up a contacts view.

We also need add, edit, and delete methods. This is done in the same way the Users methods are set up.

13. If the form has been submitted, collect the form data, perform validation, and providing there are no errors, insert it into the database, set a message, and redirect:

For full code snippet, refer to Lesson 8.php file in the code files folder.

```php
public function add()
{
......

    Session::set('success', 'Contact deleted');

    Url::redirect('/contacts');
}
```

14. Next, we need to create the views for these methods. Create a `contacts` folder inside `app/views/admin` and create these views:

 For full code snippet, refer to `Lesson 8.php` file in the code files folder.

`index.php`

```php
<?php
include(APPDIR.'views/layouts/header.php');
include(APPDIR.'views/layouts/nav.php');
.......
</form>

<?php include(APPDIR.'views/layouts/footer.php');?>
```

Activity: Executing our Application

We have implemented the CRUD functionality into our contacts application. Let's try it out by executing our application.

The aim of this activity is to verify that the CRUD functionality works properly with our application.

At this point, we can list, add, edit, and delete contacts:

1. To show this, open your application:
   ```
   php - S localhost:8000 -t webroot
   ```

2. Load up `http://localhost:8000/contacts`.

3. All contacts in the database will be listed. You can add a new one by clicking on `Add Contact`. After submitting the form, you will be taken back to the user list where you can see the new contact, and a confirmation message will be displayed.

4. The same thing will happen for editing. Deleting will confirm the action to then delete the contact.

Comments, Joins, and Date Formatting

In this section, we will learn:

- How to build a comment system
- How to join data stored in two different tables
- How to format dates

The system as it is currently built can be improved. This can be done by building a comment feature so that a user can log activity against a contact.

They may want to note that they called the contact on Monday and was asked to call them again on Friday. Users may be working together to call a list of contacts, and it would be useful to know who made that comment and when.

Another way the system can be improved is ensuring that the dates and times are displayed in an easy-to-read format. The database table stores such information in a way that is not so human-friendly.

When creating comments, it is essential to create `joins`. There is almost an unlimited amount of comments that a user can post against a contact.

It would be impossible to cater for this when building the contacts field, and the comments would have to be limited. There would need to be a field in the contacts table to cater for every possible comment, who the comment was made by, and when. This would be extremely difficult to manage and tedious to build for the developer.

Instead of having a finite amount of comments, the developer should instead create a separate table with the purpose of storing comments.

But how will the developer link the comments to the contact?

This is where `joins` become useful. Each contact has an `ID`. Each comment has a comment `ID`. Each comment also has additional information, such as the text content of the comment, who made the comment, and the time and date the comment was made.

When the comment is made by the system, it needs to be able to recognize that it is made against a specific contact and have that contact stored in that record as the contact ID.

For example, if the contact David has an ID of 1 and has three comments, then each of those comments will be stored in the table that has a contact ID of 1. They will all have unique IDs of their own, namely, 1, 2, and 3.

The same is applied to users so it is possible to know which user made the comment. This would be the user ID. The `join` is required because the comment only has limited knowledge of the user that made it and the contact it belongs to. It merely knows that the contact ID of the contact it is related to and the user ID of the user that created it.

This is fine for a computer, but a human user needs more information than this. They will want to see the name of that user, not just their ID on the system. Joining together two or three tables with all the relevant information is required to achieve this. This is an example of how the database feeds the system. A few simple PHP functions can easily reformat this data.

Database that is fed to the system:

```
2017-12-15
```

PHP can reformat this to:

```
Friday 15th December 2017
```

Creating a View Page and Building the Comments System

The purpose of this section is to show the contacts of the CRUD in operation. The following screenshot shows you what we're planning to accomplish by the end of this section.

The comments system

To make our contacts section more useful, let's add a `view` page where we can see an individual contact. The `view` page is also a perfect place to build a comments system to add comments against the contact:

1. Open your `Contacts` controller and create a new method called `view($id)`.

2. Check that the `$id` is numeric and then load the contact from `get_contact($id)`. If `$contact` is empty, redirect to a 404 page.

3. Set the page title and load the view:

```
public function view($id)
{
    if (! is_numeric($id)) {
        Url::redirect('/contacts');
    }

    $contact = $this->contact->get_contact($id);

    if ($contact == null) {
        Url::redirect('/404');
    }
```

```
    $title = 'View Contact';
    $this->view->render('admin/contacts/view', compact('contact',
'title'));
}
```

4. In `app/views/admin/contacts`, create `view.php`.

5. Load the layout files, then create a table to display the content, ensuring the variables are wrapped inside `htmlentities()`:

 For full code snippet, refer to `Lesson 8.php` file in the code files folder.

```php
<?php
include(APPDIR.'views/layouts/header.php');
include(APPDIR.'views/layouts/nav.php');
include(APPDIR.'views/layouts/errors.php');
......
</div>

<?php include(APPDIR.'views/layouts/footer.php');?>
```

6. Now, to start working on the comments, first we need a form to enter a comment and submit it. After the table but before the footer layout, create a heading called `Comments` and create a form with a single text area. Give the text area a name of body:

```html
<h1>Comments</h1>
<form method="post">
    <div class="control-group">
        <textarea class="form-control" name="body"></textarea>
    </div>
    <p><button type="submit" class="btn btn-success"
name="submit"><i class="fa fa-check"></i> Add Comment</button></p>
</form>
```

When this form is submitted, the `view` method needs to process the request.

Before we can go any further, we need a Comment model to interact with the `comments` table in the database.

7. In `app/Models`, create a new model called `Comment.php`. For now, it will
    have one method, called `insert($data)`, which will create a new record in
    the comments table when called:

```php
<?php
namespace App\Models;

use System\BaseModel;

class Comment extends BaseModel
{
    public function insert($data)
    {
        $this->db->insert('comments', $data);
    }
}
```

8. Now, go to your `Contacts` controller.

9. Import the new `Comment` model at the top of the file:

```php
use App\Models\Comment;
```

10. In the `view($id)` method, create a new instance of the Comment model.

    As this comment model will only be used in this method, we don't need to
    assign it to a class property. A local variable is fine, in this case, $comment.

11. Next, check for the form submission and collect the `$body` post data.

12. If the comment is not empty, then create a `$data` array containing the body
    but also the `contact_id`, which is the `$id`, and the `user_id`, which is the ID
    of the logged-in in user which is stored in a session.

13. Pass the `$data` to the `insert($data)` method to create the comment, and
    then set a message and redirect back to the view page of the contact:

```php
$comment = new Comment();
        if (isset($_POST['submit'])) {
            $body  = (isset($_POST['body']) ? $_POST['body'] :
null);
            if ($comment !='') {
                $data = [
                    'body' => $body,
                    'contact_id' => $id,
```

```
                              'user_id' => Session::get('user_id')
                         ];
                         $comment->insert($data);
                         Session::set('success', 'Comment created');
                         Url::redirect("/contacts/view/$id");
               }
```

Activity: Loading the Application

We have built the page and implemented the comments system. We will now load the application. After loading the application, you will notice that there is an edit and delete button, but there is no way to see that contact. We will fix this.

We'll look at enabling visibility of contacts in our application by following these steps:

1. Load up the application:

    ```
    php -S localhost:8000 -t webroot load http://localhost:8000/
    contacts
    ```

2. Have you noticed that there is an edit and delete button for each contact but no way to see the contact? Let's fix that.

3. Open `app/views/admin/contacts/index.php`.

4. Add a new link above the edit link. In this case, I've given the button a different class, `btn-info`, to make the button blue so it's different to the edit:

    ```
    <a href="/contacts/view/<?=$row->id;?>" class="btn btn-xs btn-
    info">View</a>
    ```

5. Save and reload the page in the browser and you will see the view button. Click the view button and you will see a view page showing the contact and a form to enter a comment.

6. Enter a comment and press `Add Comment`. The page will reload and you will see a success message. The comment has been inserted into the database, but you won't see it yet.

7. Open your Comment model.

8. Create a new method called `get_comments($id)`. The `$id` passed will be the ID of the contact.

For this query, we need to do a `join`.

 A join is where you join two or more database tables together to get information out of them.

We need a join to get the username of the user who added the comment. In the comments table, we store a `user_id`. This can be used to for getting anything we need from the users table.

The syntax for a `join` is to select the columns required, prefixed with the table name and followed by the comment.

So the user's username says go to the users table and fetch the `username` column.

1. In the `from` section, specify the table to load, and in the where section, specify the criteria.

2. We want to load all comments where the comments `user_id` column matches the user's ID column, and where the `contact_id` matches the provided `$id`:

```
public function get_comments($id)
{
    return $this->db->select('
        comments.body,
        comments.created_at,
        users.username
    from
        comments,
        users
    where
        comments.user_id = users.id
        and contact_id = :id'
    , [':id' => $id]);
}
```

3. Save this model and go to the `view` method of the `Contacts` controller.

4. After the form has been processed, make a call to the `get_comments($id)` method we just created:

```
$comments = $comment->get_comments($id);
```

5. This loads the comments; the next step is to add comments to the compact function:

```
$this->view->render('admin/contacts/view', compact('contact',
'comments', 'title'));
```

The full method looks like this:

 For full code snippet, refer to `Lesson 8.php` file in the code files folder.

```
public function view($id)
{
    if (! is_numeric($id)) {
        Url::redirect('/contacts');
.......
    $comments = $comment->get_comments($id);

    $title = 'View Contact';
    $this->view->render('admin/contacts/view', compact('contact',
'comments', 'title'));
}
```

6. The final step is to display the comments. Open `app/views/admin/contacts/view.php`.

7. After the form, add:

```
<?php foreach($comments as $row) { ?>
    <div class="well">
        <p><?=htmlentities($row->body);?></p>
        <p>By <?=$row->username;?> at <?=date('jS M Y H:i:s',
strtotime($row->created_at));?></p>
    </div>
<?php } ?>
```

This loops through the comments. Each loop creates a new div with a class for a bit of styling. Inside the div, it prints out the comment. On the next line, the username is displayed. The username is only available due to the join we set up in the Comment model.

1. When the comment was added, the created_at field was populated. The default format is YYYY-MM-DD H:M:S, which is not very readable, so we can use date() to specify the date format, and as a second param use strtotime() and pass in the created_at field.

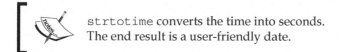

> strtotime converts the time into seconds. The end result is a user-friendly date.

2. Now, go back to a contact in your browser and add a comment. You will then see the new comment and any previous comments displayed on the page.

Summary

In this chapter, we have covered how to build CRUD sections that interact with forms, pass data from page to page and format dates. We have also added a comments system in our contacts application which can enable the users to add comments and record them.

We covered all the concepts which are required for developing a good and secure PHP application.

This concludes the book. In this book, we've learned all the basics of PHP like variables, arrays, loops, and so on. We have also learnt how to develop a PHP framework in an OOP environment while building the contacts application. We covered how the structure of a framework looks and how to properly format the error reporting technique using Whoops. Along with the framework development, we covered the authentication and user management in a framework developing environment and, finally, we covered how to CRUD our contacts application.

Index

M

mathematical operators

method 69

monthly pay of employee
calculating 46

multidimensional arrays
working with 22, 24, 25

MVC structure
about 75
working 77-80

MySQL database
connecting to 55, 56
database table, creating 56, 57
multiple rows, fetching from database
  table 59
record, deleting in database table 61-64
record, inserting 57
record, updating in database table 60
single row, fetching from database
  table 58, 59

O

object
about 69

OOP concepts
about 67
access modifiers 70
controllers 68
methods 69
namespace app 68
namespaces 67
objects, defining with namespaces 69
use statements 68

operators
comparison operators 5
logical operators 6
mathematical operators 7
using, in PHP 7

P

password hashing 133

password recovery
about 146
building 146
third party dependency PHP mailer,
  adding 147, 148

password reset mechanism
building, for application 148-155

PDO
working with 106, 107, 109

PHP
about 1
conditionals 8
data types 4
operators 5
syntax 2
variables 3

PHP MVC framework
base controller class 102
building 83, 84
configuration class 93
dependencies installation, Composer
  used 91, 92
error handling, Composer used 85-91
error handling, Whoops used 85
model, creating 119, 120
PDO, working with 106
project development environment, setting
  up 84
results, exploring 105
route class 94

PHP web application
building 65
Contact model 73, 74
contacts, adding to directory 80-82
file structure 71
MVC structure, using 66, 67

R

raw method 110

S

select method 110

simple function
  creating 39

slicing arrays 21

sticky forms 160

syntax, PHP
  about 2
  example 2, 3

T

truncate method 114, 115

U

update method 113

V

variables
  about 3
  implementing 4, 5

variables, and conditionals
  using 12, 13

W

while loops
  example 28
  working with 28

Whoops library
  about 85
  used, for error handling in PHP MVC
      framework 85

Made in the USA
Coppell, TX
10 January 2020